Personality Portraits
The Enneagram Encountered

Amanda Maney & Rachel Watson

Enneagram Insights
Publishing

Published in 2014 by

Enneagram Insights
Publishing

www.powerofpersonality.com

© & ℗ Copyright Amanda Maney and Rachel Watson 2014

ISBN: 978-0-9930852-2-2

Conditions of sale

This book is sold subject to the condition that it shall not, by way of trade or otherwise, be lent, re-sold, hired out or otherwise circulated without the publisher's prior consent in any form or binding other than that which it is published and without a similar condition including this condition being imposed on the subsequent purchaser. All rights reserved.

For everyone!

Contents

Foreword	1
Prefaces	5
Introduction	9
Values - What makes people tick?	17
Three centres: heart, head & gut	27
Type Two - The Helper	35
Type Three - The Achiever	45
Type Four - The Individualist	55
Type Five - The Forensic	65
Type Six - The Teammate	75
Type Seven - The Adventurer	85
Type Eight - The Champion	95
Type Nine - The Peacemaker	105
Type One - The Reformer	115
Painting by numbers	125
Author Biographies	128

Foreword

Foreword

As a publisher and author of self-help and transformation books, I see countless different manuscripts in the course of a year. Some are inspiring and interesting reads. Others have the capacity to make a difference in the lives of a number of people. Then there are the books that are truly transformational.

In order for a book of this nature to be transformational, it needs to take the reader beyond where they can go themselves. It needs to be able to skilfully shake up the way the reader sees the world. It needs to enable them to reach a place that they might not necessarily have been able to reach on their own. This book does exactly that.

If you are holding this book in your hands, you have probably already been struck by the uniqueness and beauty of its design. But this book goes way beyond being an eye-catching and visually stunning product.

The uniqueness of this book lies firstly in the accessibility of the information shared within. Over the years, many people who I respect have enthusiastically shared their love and passion for the Enneagram with me. And I have to say that although I am well versed in the personal development and transformation industry, the Enneagram is something that I've never really understood. Everything that was put in front of me seemed complicated and overly formulaic. That is until I encountered this book. Even just flicking through it in the first ten minutes gave me more understanding that I had gleaned in hours of previous study.

Two of the key things that this book gives its readers are self-acceptance and self-awareness. Many of the traits that the reader may have previously considered as flaws, are turned on their head as being unique character traits. With this new level of awareness comes a greater sense of self-acceptance. This ultimately creates a powerful opportunity for growth, learning and expansion.

The other great thing about this book is that it is highly interactive. So many books fail their readers because they don't give them anything to do in the real world. This book enables the readers to take what they have learned out into their lives, bringing the theories and concepts alive.

This is the book that newcomers can pick up, with no knowledge or experience of the Enneagram, and instantly recognise themselves in. It's the book that practitioners of this modality can give to their clients to support the work they are doing. It's the book that more experienced enthusiasts will keep to hand, to reinforce and support the love for that which they hold dear. Whether you are just starting out, a seasoned practitioner, or wanting to introduce someone you care about to the Enneagram, this book is a powerful resource that you will use again and again.

Sasha Allenby – co-author of Matrix Reimprinting Using EFT, ghostwriter, CEO of Wisdompreneurs Publishing

Prefaces

Prefaces

When first encountering the Enneagram in the late 1980s, I found it mind-blowing - such a revelation - this wisdom seemed to be describing me from the inside out. Following my reading with a five day workshop gave me even more. In one instant of absolute truth, every millisecond of my life was explained to me: in that moment I understood EVERYTHING - every choice, from parking spaces to dog food; my dress sense, my speaking style - EVERYTHING!

What did this truth do for me? Well, it allowed me to stop beating myself up for the multitude of character defects I perceived within myself. It was such liberation to realise that my 'flaws' were actually typical of my personality type - I was not alone in my struggle to be 'better' and 'more'.

But more than that, it introduced me to the concept that these 'failings' were, in fact, the reverse of the coin, as it were, to my strengths. Strengths! Now that was a foreign concept at that time! Compassion and appreciation - for self and others - flows so naturally from this work. It is transformational and a huge joy to share.

I am intensely grateful to those who brought me to the Enneagram in the first place - my dear friend Lucy Brill, Brandon Bays and Sr Elizabeth McNulty who shared their understanding so generously and skilfully. I also want to thank Rachel Watson for developing this passion with me, and her whole family for entering into the project with such aplomb and pizzazz! And deep thanks to all those who have worked with us with such honesty and courage, sharing their own stories and struggles, bringing us all to greater understanding of the wisdom and truth that is the Enneagram.

Amanda

With a corporate background, I had become familiar with many personality descriptors and whilst I found them interesting and useful, I was always left with the feeling...so what? And what do I do now?

When introduced to the Enneagram by Amanda, I was instantly blown away by the depth and breadth that the Enneagram provided to help us understand other people. I was hooked!

As my experience and knowledge grew, I became fascinated and amazed by how useful this tool was becoming in its insight - into myself, my husband, my children, family, friends and clients and why I connected so easily with some people whilst others were a little more of a challenge.

My family now have an in-depth understanding of the Enneagram, which has helped them to truly understand themselves and each other and has proven valuable in their professional lives. On a personal level, I believe we are more compassionate as a family because we truly understand each other.

This tool for compassion enhances my work massively and fuels my interest in people and how they operate.

I would like to thank all the people who have attended our workshops and generously shared their stories. A particular thanks goes to all those who have kindly taken the time to write down their stories and who have shared their experiences so happily for the benefit of this book and its readers. I am forever grateful to you all.

Rachel

Our promise to you:

This book will introduce you to yourself and to others through fresh perspectives and deep questions; completing the accompanying exercises is guaranteed to enhance your experience of life and relationships.

Enjoy!

Please note that the celebrity quotations used with the chapter headings for the nine types are offered as exemplars of each type's way of thinking; they are not categorising or typing the celebrities themselves.
The other quotations used throughout the chapters are from course delegates who have given us permission to share these thoughts in order to illustrate the different characteristics of each type.

The Enneagram Encountered

An Introduction

What is the Enneagram?

The Enneagram (the name is from two Greek words - 'ennea', meaning nine and 'grammos', meaning something written or drawn) has its origins in oral traditions, which span centuries and offers profound insights into the ways personality can affect and direct us without our conscious awareness. The Enneagram describes nine distinct personality types simply numbered 1-9, each one driven, subconsciously, by the need to avoid an emotion perceived at a primal level to be life threatening. Reading about the Enneagram - its history and evolution - is fascinating for those who enjoy research and there is now a plethora of books available to give you such information. That, however, is **not** what this book is for.

So, what is this book for?

The intention of this book is not just to tell you about the Enneagram, more to invite you *into* it. The Enneagram holds profound truth for those who enjoy its organic approach, but it needs experience and dialogue to fully access this truth. We like to say that the Enneagram is like an impressionist painting: it is so much more than a painting by numbers exercise, it is full of colour and nuance and deep meaning, but enigmatic, subtle and elusive. The deeper you delve, the more apparent contradictions you will find. These are like blobs of colour, which make sense when you step back but seem to have no right to their place in the painting when under close scrutiny. There are many different interpretations in the books on this subject, we will offer still more... And yet, the truth within it has massive impact, unlocking relationships on a daily basis as people ***put it to use***. Comments such as: 'Now I can enjoy my children', 'The Enneagram saved my marriage' or, sadly 'If I had known about the Enneagram then I would still *be* married', are common amongst our delegates.

Our aim is to give you a working understanding of the nine personality types, ***so that you can use it*** to improve your own experience and enhance your interactions with others. This is primarily a tool for compassion and appreciation. Through it, the 'personalisation' of our own and other people's unhealthy behaviour is dissolved, to be replaced by compassion for the common pain that causes it. Understanding the Enneagram types enables you to celebrate and work to your strengths, and help others to do the same.

Frequently asked questions

Are the numbers anything to do with numerology?

Not at all, they are completely separate ideas and concepts. The nine types are given the numbers 1-9 as a simple labelling tool. Working out your type is about forming a deep understanding of the drives and motivations of each type and finding matches with your own inner drives, it cannot be worked out by any formula.

Nature or nurture?
Do we change personality types?

The Enneagram premise is that personality is inbuilt from conception and remains our type, but is massively influenced by environment, upbringing etc. We can operate very differently from our type's typical patterns if we are so influenced by strong environmental and/or nurturing factors or if we choose to make conscious change. Looking at the way twins develop tells us that there must be something other than nurture determining personality traits and outcomes, which can appear very distinctly different from the first days or weeks of life.

Aren't personality descriptors limiting? How can every person be categorised as a 'type' or put into a box?

There are many layers to the personality types, giving rise to infinite variation within each type. Two people who appear to be very different in behaviour may share the same Enneagram type, as the drivers of their behaviour are the same. Similarly, two who appear to have similar behaviours may be doing them for very different reasons and be quite different types on the Enneagram. One example of this would be two people who find it impossible to say 'no', who need to provide for others' needs even to the point of self neglect. The surface behaviours of the two might appear almost identical, but for one personality type, the drive is to be acknowledged, to be needed: a desire for love. The other personality type is actually driven by such a need to avoid conflict that keeping others happy becomes a key strategy: this is a desire for control.

How is the Enneagram different from other personality sorters?

This is a very general question, but basically the Enneagram is very different from any personality system which relies solely on questionnaires, processing of scores and a final, cut and dried outcome. Whilst that type of personality descriptor can be of value and delivers swift, clear results, this approach goes much deeper than the surface behaviours and involves a more thorough understanding of 'why' rather than 'what' we do. There are Enneagram questionnaires designed to help you type yourself; we suggest that these are useful only up to a point - it is not easy to get under the surface using questionnaires alone.

Typing yourself

This book will, for some, result in a clear and definite 'hit' as a personality type fits with uncanny accuracy and suddenly every moment of your existence makes sense - this can take your breath away.
You do need to be aware of how powerful the Enneagram can be and the impact it can have on your system. For others, reading and viewing this material will eliminate some types and suggest others, but not give certainty about the one type for you. That powerful 'lightbulb moment' of absolute recognition, when the 'penny drops' as it were, can never be guaranteed within the remit of a text such as this, although it is precisely that visceral, undeniable experience of truth which lies at the heart of the Enneagram for those who pursue it. All we would say to you is: keep seeking, stay open, be playful with all of this; sometimes these moments of clarity sneak up when you are least expecting them.

Typing others

If you enjoy the Enneagram and whether or not you have found your own type, you will inevitably find yourself typing others. Some of the people in your life will appear to leap off the pages and declare themselves to you by their behaviours.

Take care with this, you cannot get inside another's psyche to see the emotional drivers for yourself, you cannot presume accuracy. More importantly - the Enneagram gives powerful and sometimes very poignant suggestions as to our hidden, unconscious drives and motivations. These are hidden for good reason. Until or unless someone chooses to explore them it can be highly inappropriate and even damaging to try and offer information of this depth and potency. (You can lose friends over this stuff. Seriously, tread carefully!)

With this proviso in mind, the Enneagram will definitely offer insights which allow you to identify key behaviours. This will enable you to work more effectively with them and bring the best out of situations where they arise.

Why typing is tricky by text alone

Reading books and completing questionnaires will offer fascinating insights, for sure and have great value in terms of raising awareness as the possible subtleties of the subconscious, but the whole premise of the Enneagram is that our personalities are constructed by that subconscious as a way to avoid specific emotions. This avoidance can be deeply buried and may be the last thing we suspect consciously.

Hence the need for live demonstration and interaction to tease out the truths we might be hiding from ourselves. Whilst nothing will come close to exploring the Enneagram through interactive dialogue (for our next training dates see www.powerofpersonality.com)
- and there are an increasing number of courses available to do just that, we have distilled the experience our two day course offers into a book format with the supporting online resources to add depth to the descriptions offered (see www.powerofpersonality.com for more information regarding resources).

What you will definitely get from this book...

Whether or not you feel certain of your type after thoroughly exploring this book, these materials will definitely offer you plenty of food for thought, raising questions for you about your own and others' behaviours.

Understanding alone is powerful, but it inevitably leads to a desire to **do something** with it. Each personality type has potential for great strengths and giftedness. Each type also has the capacity for disintegration or mentally and emotionally unhealthy states, when out of balance or under stress. **Our types do not define us**. They just give us an awareness of why some things might be more of a challenge, what our subconscious hidden agenda might be. This knowledge gives us power to break free, power to do things differently. There is more to life than painting by numbers….

How the book is organised

The Enneagram Encountered

Values

We start by looking at values that raise our awareness of the different influences which will be operating on us at any one time. This begins the process of tuning yourself into the possible layers of motivation within you. Some values you hold dear will almost inevitably have stemmed from external influence. Others will be more core - these are the ones which will lead you home.

The three centres

We then introduce you to the three centres from which the nine types arise. Don't be tempted to miss this bit, it becomes vital in distinguishing between possibilities later and is the core to understanding the whole thing.

The types introduced

Each type is then described, using words, pictures and online resources to add depth and clarity. As you read through, try not to 'land' initially. We can all relate to elements of each personality type; just keep an open mind, notice what connects and what doesn't. Circle your metaphorical aeroplane a good few times and make sure you explore all runways before you make any conscious decision about which feels like home.

Coaching exercises

After each Enneagram type is described in the book, you will find a coaching exercise specifically designed to assist it. All the exercises are beneficial to everyone, but will have added value for that particular type.

There's more to life than painting by numbers

We finish this book (the first of our series) by bringing you back to the vital understanding that these personality descriptors – whilst potentially life changing in their accuracy and impact – are **not** who we are. There is a danger that, seeing our core drives explained so powerfully, we feel defined by them, incapable of breaking free of the patterns we see laid out before us.

Whilst the Enneagram teaches that our core personality does not change, our responses and behaviours and the people we choose to be, absolutely **can** and **do** change – potentially far more radically when we become aware of our subconscious motivations. We leave the reader with the assurance that there **is** more to life than painting by numbers, but until we are aware of those numbers, those personality patterns, we can limit ourselves to doing just that. The Enneagram frees us to choose our own destiny – to mix our own shades of paint as it were – to be free.

Summary

We have seen repeated, sustained impact and value flow from these materials as we use them with professionals, with teams, with children and families. The Enneagram is a profound and beautiful vehicle for the appreciation and celebration of human personality in all its richness and diversity.

No longer do we stand bewildered, wondering how someone else could operate so differently from ourselves. Our maps of the world are inherently different and we all need each other. The Enneagram explains those very different maps to us and shows us how to benefit from the differences we see. Teams and families benefit from the inclusion and the appreciation of all - especially those who bring challenge. The Enneagram shows us how to acknowledge and enjoy ourselves, our colleagues and our loved ones, frailties and strengths alike.

A word of warning

With the premise of the Enneagram being one of compulsively avoiding negative emotion, it is easier to spot our unconscious sub-routines when we are most unhealthy or out of balance.

This means that to explore this material, we will have to guide you to look at the downside, the pitfalls of each type, taking you back to your least healthy times to get an idea of your type. This may sound negative but, that is ***not*** our intention - as previously stated - ALL types are equally glorious in their healthy states.

The Enneagram enables us to bring our unconsciously driven limiting behaviours into the light - *so that we can make empowered, compassionate, conscious decisions about how we choose to act in the future.*

If you have decided to continue, you have a treat ahead of you - enjoy!

Values
What makes you tick?

Values – what makes you tick?

Why is it that with some people you 'click' and connect instantly - quite literally within seconds of first meeting them - whilst with others you may have known for years the conversation and connection is always just a little bit harder?

We would suggest that our ease of connection is hugely influenced by the values we hold and how compatible these are with the values of others. Our values drive and inspire us, they underpin all our decisions and choices. They make us 'tick'. The extraordinary thing is that most of us go through our entire lives without stopping to think what our values might actually be!

As a result, values are driving most people subconsciously. Most of us don't realise that our emotional reactions to people and things are reflecting our value systems back to us. Whether a relationship or life event feels like pure elation or deadly slog is very often down to whether or not that relationship or event is in line with our values.

Values and goals

If you have ever found you have set yourself goals and met them, but don't feel a great sense of satisfaction, it could well be because your goals are not in line with your values. Likewise, when goals *are* in line with values, something small and comparatively insignificant can leave you feeling elated! Your goals should underpin your values, not the other way around. Many organisations are now establishing values from which their goals are being set and are even recruiting staff based on these values. Dating agencies are now matching couples based on values!

Some people say their values change - perhaps they do on occasion, particularly through life changing/dramatic events. We think the sense of changing values is generally more to do with the fact that at a particular moment in time, our values may be being dishonoured, or we are less satisfied with how our values are being met at that moment in time, thus emphasising some values or de-emphasising others. When we are really clear about our values and they are being met on a consistent and regular basis, life feels good - really good. We feel inspired, we feel motivated, we feel 'in the flow' of life.

Understanding your values takes time; it is not something you can necessarily do in one sitting, but it is definitely time well spent. In truly understanding your values you can set your life up consciously to optimise the fantastic buzz that alignment with your values can give, living very deliberately in the flow of life, swimming with the current as it were, rather than struggling upstream.

Some people like to have separate 'personal' and 'work' values and that is absolutely fine. We actually see our values as 'life' values, because all of life is important and what's truly important transcends the whole of life.

Unique to you

We are individuals and our own maps of the world are personalised and unique. It therefore stands to reason that our own set of values will also be unique.
Often, however, when we come to look at this fundamental aspect of life, we discover that we have actually acquired the values of others along the way…our parents, siblings, peers, mentors, teachers etc.
So many times we have heard people say when working through the values exercise…
"Those are not my values – they're my parents' values!"

It is only when we stop and consider: "Who am I?" "What really makes me tick?" "How do I want to show up in the world?" "What is truly important to me?" Only then can we start to define our own values, rather than being governed by the values we think we 'should' have or even would like to have… Then we can start to become truly authentic.

Values are not about who we think we should be or even who we would like to be, but a reflection of who we **actually** are.

When we ask people to define their values, we exclude the words… 'family', 'work' and 'money' because we want people to define what it is about family, work and money that is important.

If we were to ask a room full of people 'What is it about work that is important to you?'… we would probably receive a whole host of responses… fulfilment, financial security, a sense of achievement, team work and fun…
We need to get to the true values underlying these major elements of life to understand why people may have such a range of different responses to them.

Creating a fulfilling life

When helping people to clarify their values, often there will be a 'light bulb moment' - a sudden clarity as to why things are working, or not, in their lives. Understanding values enables them to create more meaning and satisfaction both at work and at home.

For instance, a person who might value both 'financial security' and 'helping others' might be increasingly frustrated with a job enabling the former but not the latter. The person has no desire to move away from a financially secure job, but is not overtly involved in helping others. Knowing the values-based cause of the resulting dissatisfaction would empower that person to make other choices to honour the 'helping others' value: e.g. taking up a mentoring role or engaging in charity work.

Life has more meaning and fulfilment when our values are being met. We can become quite creative about how to achieve this fulfilment. We do not have to have all values met in any one arena or relationship. This information can be crucial to enhancing happiness and performance.

Easing interactions

We believe that when we truly know what we value, it becomes easier to appreciate the values of others. This naturally increases our capacity for compassion and understanding. So rather than thinking, "Why can't they see it my way?"… "Why do they **do** that?"… "How can they feel or think like that?"…

We can let go and become more tolerant.
It takes the heat out of challenging situations with others knowing that it's just that THEIR map of the world is different: they see, hear and feel things differently because what they value is different - not better, not worse, just different.

The following exercise will help you to understand what makes you tick and what is important to you. It can also help you uncover which personality type you may be, as certain values will resonate with some 'types' more than others.

This will help to clarify for you, why the 'dance' with some people is easier than others, because you have similar values to them or their values complement your own. Think about those closest to you, those people with whom you get along so easily... Could they have similar or complementary values to you? The likelihood is that they will.

If we lose sight of our values, we can lose sight of our true identity. Sometimes it can be easier to define our lives in terms of what we do, rather than who we are and what motivates us. When we have established our values, it can be a powerful aid to making life choices, particularly when we are at a crossroads in our lives.

Take time to complete and enjoy the Values exercise.

Values exercise

Write down your top ten work values and your top ten personal values (some may be the same). On the opposite page we have listed some values to get you started - don't let our list restrict you - it is far from comprehensive!

If you think of words such as 'family', 'work or 'money', consider: What do family, work and money mean to you? What do they represent? What do they give you?

If you wish, combine your work and personal values to establish your overall top ten life values and prioritise them. Then, for each of your top ten life values, write one sentence saying why they are important. For instance:

Independence – having the freedom to make choices and decisions, being self sufficient and self reliant

Achievement- for my life and work to have a feeling of fulfilment, serving others and serving my own desires and needs

Love & passion – excited in all I do, having variety in my life, sharing this passion and love with those around me, when life is joyful, full of warmth and enthusiasm and I have a zest for life

truth, achievement, flexibility, integrity, justice, peace of mind, fulfilment, innovation, freedom, strength, teamwork, autonomy, sincerity, compassion, perspective, independence, dependability, passion, excitement, challenge, empowerment, love, security, self-control, self-respect, patience, humour, peace, commitment, recognition, excellence, personal development, friendship, balance, health, responsibility, fairness, diligence, efficiency, loyalty, spirituality, fun, adventure, creativity, success, trust, learning, helping others, risk taking, honesty, fame, financial security, courage

(add your own if different)

Compassion – being tender, kind, loving and empathetic to myself, my family, friends, clients and the world around me.

Next:
See how well your values are being met at the moment by scoring each one on a scale of 1-10; with 1 being not satisfied at all, and 10 being totally satisfied. Identify areas you wish to improve. Determine what actions or small steps you will take to improve your scores….

WORK VALUES

Value	Define what this value means to you	Current level of satisfaction 1-10

PERSONAL VALUES

Value	Define what this value means to you	Current level of satisfaction 1-10

REFLECTION

What has this exercise revealed to you?

What actions could you take to raise your satisfaction levels?

Do by date: when might you do this?

The three centres

The three centres: heart, head and gut

The nine personality types described by the Enneagram reside in three centres, each centre with three types within it, being driven by the need to avoid one particular feeling.

The three personality types within each centre respond to this need in very different ways, but they have certain things in common because they are sponsored by the same fundamental avoidance: the emotion they are avoiding drives their personality and the behaviours that arise from it.

When trying to distinguish core motivations, the Enneagram involves getting *beneath* behaviours to find out *why* they are happening: this understanding is crucial. As previously stated, identical behaviours can come from completely different centres and equally, the same centre can produce very different looking behaviours.

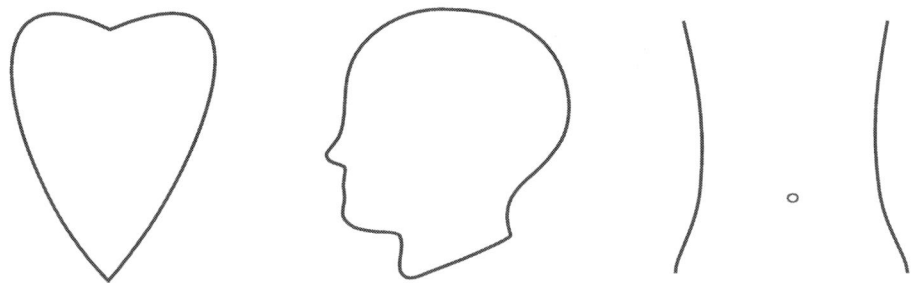

Key principles of the centres:

The three centres are known as the **heart, head and gut centres**.

The 'driven-ness' of the types is utterly subconscious.

'Heart' types are driven by a feeling of **hurt** or **shame**, producing a need for **love** and **acknowledgment**.

'Head' or 'mind' types are driven by **fear**, creating a need for **safety**.

'Gut' types are driven by **anger**, which results in a need for **control**.

The following statements are broad brush strokes in our painting - get a general feel for them, but don't hang anything up on any one statement. We can all do some of all of this - we act from all three centres which gives our personality balance and health...
But one centre will be 'home'.

Have a think about your own responses and reactions: which of the three emotions are you most/least comfortable with?

Hurt?/Shame?
Fear?
Anger?

If one of these were driving you, which one do you think it would be?

What answers would others who know you well give?

Heart types - 2,3,4

The Enneagram proposes that the heart types subconsciously feel unloved as they enter the world. They feel that somehow they must acquire love, that it will not come to them naturally, that they are somehow unworthy of love in the eyes of others.

Knowing that love is necessary for life, their behaviours therefore develop with the one aim - to be loved (or at least noticed, some heart types have subconsciously given up on the notion of actual 'love').

We refer to 'having the heart' to do things, or being 'all heart' - this is the centre of emotion. Access to this centre is crucial to any team - if the heart is not engaged, all the mind's plans and the gut's actions will count for nothing - we will find ourselves having climbed a great ladder, reaching the top to discover that it was placed against the wrong wall!

Heart types when out of balance will paradoxically struggle most with emotion - becoming 'heartless' in their responses to life. They need help to access, value and balance their feelings and to love themselves for who they are.

Energy levels

The heart types tend to have quite steady energy levels - rather like the circulatory system, pacing itself and keeping going at a fairly even output most of the time.

Thinking style

The main thinking type attributed to the heart types is network 'joined up' thinking - the type that creates rapid connection in many different directions at once. This type of thinking enables heart types to see in an instant all the ramifications inherent in any given situation. Heart types are said to be mostly focused on the present moment - they are less happy to plan and do not spend as much time reflecting on past experiences but want to work fresh from minute to minute with a clean mental slate.

We would suggest that the heart centre is the seat of **impulse**. We talk about letting our hearts override our heads, following our heart etc. The heart types are oriented towards discerning **'good'** from **'bad'**.

Key (subconscious) question

The subconscious of the heart types is always asking **'Who am I?'** They search for relationship and acknowledgement from their environment.

Clarifying question

How **needy** are you?

The heart types, when unhealthy will move **towards** others in their need for love/attention - others will perceive this as cloying, needy, suffocating or emotionally draining.

Head types - 5,6,7

The head types subconsciously fear the world. They perceive that the world is a dangerous place and that they are unsafe. Their behaviours become constructed around this one, over-riding premise, their prime directive, as it were - to be safe.

As the brain and nervous system are protected by bone, so the head types strive, through their behaviour, to protect themselves from the world's many threats and perils.

We talk about head types being 'cerebral', about being able to 'do anything we put our mind to' - it is the centre for planning and decision making - the centre of knowing. Once again, however, despite this being the gift of the head types, when unhealthy, this is the very thing they will tend to struggle with most, losing focus and backing off, 'witless' as it were, detaching themselves from life.

Energy levels

The head types tend to have quite high energy levels - it can be like electrical energy, fast and at times quite frenetic or nervous, but cutting out rather abruptly when depleted.

Thinking style

The main thinking type attributed to the head types is logical, progressive thinking - the type that leads to focused specialism in one or more specific fields. This is the most natural realm of the academic, the researcher, the specialised genius. (Remember, broad brush strokes - this does not mean that all genius lies here!) Head types are more likely to spend higher proportions of time thinking about the future, planning, speculating, imagining and worrying about what might be.

We would suggest that the head centre is the seat of **intuition**. We talk about picking up on 'vibes', about having a sense of 'knowing' about something which cannot be rationally explained. The head types are oriented towards discerning **'true'** from **'false'**.

Key (subconscious) question

The subconscious of the head types is always asking **'Where am I?'** - gauging and assessing potential risks in the current environment.

Clarifying question

How *fearful* are you?

The head types, when unhealthy, will move **away from** others in their need for security - others will perceive this as being distant, brusque, disconnected, edgy.

Gut types - 8,9,1

The gut types subconsciously rage against the world. They perceive that they have come into the world vulnerable and unprotected. Rather than fearing the world, their subconscious rails against it and their behaviours become constructed around an over-riding need to control their environment.

The gut is the least protected part of the body, hence the rage. It is also the place in the body associated with raw courage, we talk about having 'the guts', or not being able to 'stomach' something - it is the power centre. When out of balance, gut types feel disempowered or 'gutless' (though they may appear to others to be quite the opposite) and become more and more desperate to control their environment as a result.

Energy levels

The gut types tend to have bursts of energy, like the movements of the alimentary tract - more of an uneven, spiky profile with major highs and lows - they are often aware of needing to conserve energy and can feel quite edgy if they feel that situations or people are draining them.

Thinking style

The main thinking type attributed to the gut types is analogous, pattern seeking thinking - using comparison to find meaning and create solutions. Metaphorical, figurative approaches often result from this type of thinking. Gut types are often disposed to dwelling on past experiences, seeking wisdom from their history, trying to use it to control the present and future. We would suggest that the gut centre is the seat of **instinct**. We talk about consulting our guts to get an instant 'yes' or 'no' about situations, this is a felt, solid certainty, which has no need for thought, rationalisation or logic. The gut types are oriented towards discerning **'right'** from **'wrong'**.

Key (subconscious) question

The subconscious of the gut types is always asking **'How am I?'** - gauging and assessing how well the environment is meeting their needs - for gut types, survival is key.

Clarifying question

How *controlling* are you?

The gut types, when unhealthy, will move **against** others in their need for control - others will perceive this as bullying, manipulative or stubborn.

The nine types

2 The Helper

"Being unwanted, unloved, uncared for, forgotten by everyone, I think that is a much greater hunger, a much greater poverty than the person who has nothing to eat."

Mother Teresa, Roman Catholic nun, founder of the Missionaries of Charity, recipient of Nobel Peace Prize 1979

Caring, empathetic, loving nurturers, 2s are generous, warm and friendly, always on the look-out for opportunities to serve; they want to know they are needed.

"I would do anything to help anyone in any situation and almost automatically know what it is that they need."

2s are the first of the heart centre types, searching for love by meeting the needs of others. 2s are driven to make themselves indispensable - the affection and appreciation they get in return provides the love they subconsciously seek. Core values for the 2 are likely to include: love, helping others, dependability and appreciation.

"I am generally a cup half-full person: making friends and building relationships come naturally."

When in balance, 2s are enthusiastic, encouraging and upbeat. They have a gift for sensing needs in any situation and giving of themselves unstintingly in their desire to fill those needs. 2s are welcoming and approachable, they invite you to ask them for help, making you feel really comfortable asking - you can sense the real pleasure it gives them. They go to great lengths to help people feel good; they delight in drawing people in and building them up.

"I get huge satisfaction from helping others. 'Busy, busy, busy' describes me well. At different times in my life I've been: a Brownie leader, a helper at clubs, a school governor and a teenage mentor."

On a good day!

2s' generosity in the service of others is boundless: they are ready to make great sacrifices to fulfill the needs they perceive. They thrive in the serving and helping roles and professions: some in the classic role of mother, nurse, teacher, therapist; others in that of the indispensible executive personal assistant. Coupled with this there is an undeniable strength to the 2 – they are determined and focused - there is a power to their purpose.

"When you need him, he will pull out all the stops. He is the man to know if you ever have a problem because even if he doesn't have the answer he will know someone who does, he will never say 'No'."

The drive for love of the heart centre fuels tireless 'labours of love' – busy, constantly extending themselves for others, preemptive providers; they need you to know they will ALWAYS be there for you.

"In the last few months alone, he has: run to help someone jump start a car, given a child a plaster, spotted someone only last week whose glasses only had one nose piece – he was able to produce a spare nose piece and screw driver and was able to fix her glasses on the spot. All this is due to his uncanny ability to have every item of appropriate equipment in his pocket, just in case it should be needed."

On a bad day!

Hidden behind these apparently selfless acts of kindness is an agenda unrecognized by an unhealthy 2; the compulsion to provide for others' needs gives them the illusion that they have no needs of their own – creating a sense of pride and superiority. In fact, quite the reverse is true. The whole pattern is driven by their overwhelming need for love and acknowledgement. This becomes apparent when they do not receive the attention they seek. Out of balance 2s become manipulative and hysterical in their desperation to be appreciated.

"I resent it if I think I am there for others more than they are for me, or something I've done hasn't been recognized or appreciated... As my children get older I can feel a rising panic about the day they leave home. It's crazy, but I'm welling up even writing this. I know I'll feel lost without them around and it'll be a huge transition for me."

Subconsciously, an unhealthy 2 will do everything possible to encourage dependency, which feeds their sense of indispensability and value – they feel loved when people cannot manage without them. Being surplus to requirement is an absolute anathema to a 2; when it happens to them it is devastating and can cause manic neediness – the 2 becomes clinging and desperate for reassurance. This often creates the opposite response from others, who instinctively draw away.

"I feel abandoned by everyone even though they were not aware they should be needing my help. I feel totally lost and useless."

"I can be prone to slight exaggeration and ... being too helpful can be annoying to some. I can fall into the 'martyr' role... I think 'less is more' should be one of my philosophies."

2s are seduced by whatever cause will give them the greatest sense of acknowledgement in any given situation. There is no coming between a 2 and the person or event offering the 'loudest' appreciation. They cannot say 'No' to a plea which offers strong gratitude – they will neglect their own and even others' needs in their pursuit of the 'love' they feel they receive - and deserve - from one who overtly depends upon them. Health, diet, sleep, finances, friendships, wellbeing – all are sacrificed for the sake of 'love'.

"I used to be extremely independent, whereas now I cannot use a DVD player, camera, set up a new 'phone, due to my (2) husband... doing everything for me. On the way to a Parent Teachers' Association committee meeting, I warned him not to go overboard in helping as I was genuinely concerned we may have ended up holding the summer fair in our own back garden!"

Recognizing the selfishness of their 'selflessness', whether at a conscious or subconscious level, allows 2s to release others from the strings of being required to give effusive thankful responses. They can enjoy their immense capacity to love and support others for the sheer pleasure of giving – not needing to receive adulation in response. This opens the channels of natural appreciation and they thrive.

"Until a few years ago, I didn't really have any hobbies to speak of… but as my children have got older and don't need or rely on me as much I have got myself some hobbies and am managing to enjoy them without feeling guilty."

"Knowing I am a 2 has helped me understand that when I offer to help with something but I am not needed, it is not because of me. This has helped reduce the hurt I would normally have felt."

The Golden Labrador is the epitome of the 2:
Loving and loyal, the Golden Labrador has limitless energy for love and affection and a unique instinct for tuning in to the needs of those they serve.

Core values for the 2 are likely to include:
love, helping others, dependability and appreciation.

Powerful and strong – their love has boundless breadth – 2s have the capacity to love the unlovable; they challenge us to open our hearts to embrace and meet the needs of all.

Coaching technique: The rocking chair

This exercise is beneficial to everyone, but is particularly useful for Type 2s, who are constantly considering the needs of others rather than their own.

If you find this is a difficult exercise to complete you may have an affinity with the Type 2 personality. Type 9s will often struggle with this exercise too, but for a different reason - Type 2s have to consider others' needs before their own in order to feel loved, Type 9s generally feel they have to go with other people's preferences in order to keep the peace, so they can lose any sense of their own desires.

Most of us are so busy reacting to what life seems to throw at or demand from us, that we don't take the time to consider what we actually want to do with our lives. We hear the expression, 'Life is not a rehearsal' but we don't stop to plan for the things we really want to achieve or experience. We may then find ourselves regretting those missed opportunities, the dreams we didn't dare to follow.

Research shows that people who write down their desires in life are statistically far more likely to achieve them than those who do not write them down. Take the time now: give yourself permission
– indulgent though it might seem – to really think about what you want from life, by following this simple exercise.

Imagine you are 100 years old, sitting in your rocking chair on your patio reviewing your life. Imagine that your life has been totally fulfilling and satisfying – that it has been everything you could possibly have wanted it to be.

What memories would you like to be pondering?

What pictures would you like to have in your mind's eye?

What would you be saying about yourself and your life?

What would others be saying about you?

What would you like to have done?

What achievements would be making you proud?

What places would you like to have visited?

What relationships would you like to have built?

How will you feel?

What person would you like to have become?

You could turn this into a 'To do, be and have' list of all the things you want to do be and have in life, perhaps even adding timeframes for the achievement of each one. This will really bring your desires into focus for you.

The rocking chair

What memories would you like to be pondering?

What pictures would you like to have in your mind's eye?

What would you be saying about yourself and your life?

What would others be saying about you?

What would you like to have done?

What achievements would be making you proud?

What places would you like to have visited?

What relationships would you like to have built?

How will you feel?

What person would you like to have become?

REFLECTION

What has this exercise revealed to you?

What actions could you take to make the most of this exercise?

Do by date: when might you do this?

The Achiever

"I touch things and people say they turn to gold...
It's a natural instinct."

Lord Alan Sugar
English business magnate, media personality, and political advisor

Accomplished, efficient, image-orientated performers, 3s are charismatic and engaging, busy with their drive to achieve, they want you to notice their shiny success.

"My parents tell stories of my formative years and they forever cite my true 3 style first words, 'Look at me'."

"When I am ... healthy ... I am very energetic and efficient. I remain upbeat and optimistic and have a positive view of life. I am very driven to achieve the best in all I do. I am also competitive and hard working. I am good at motivating people when necessary."

3s are the second of the heart centre types, searching for love but trying to get it in very different ways from the 2. Whilst 2s attempt to gain love by being needed, 3s have **subconsciously** given up on being loved and they seek respect as a substitute. 3s become focused then on creating an image of success in their chosen fields, not necessarily involving money or the usual trappings of that success. Core values for the 3 are likely to include: success, achievement, efficiency and acknowledgement.

"Working in front of a camera in television was my dream job and although I have done many interesting things - including working in live radio and as a reporter on a local newspaper - my TV presenting work is undoubtedly my 3 working wonderfully. No fear of being a 'nobody'."

At their best, 3s are charming, inspiring and self assured. They are practical and focused, there is a 'buzz' about them, an energy that draws others in; they attract the skills and talents of others, they can create and motivate massively productive teams.

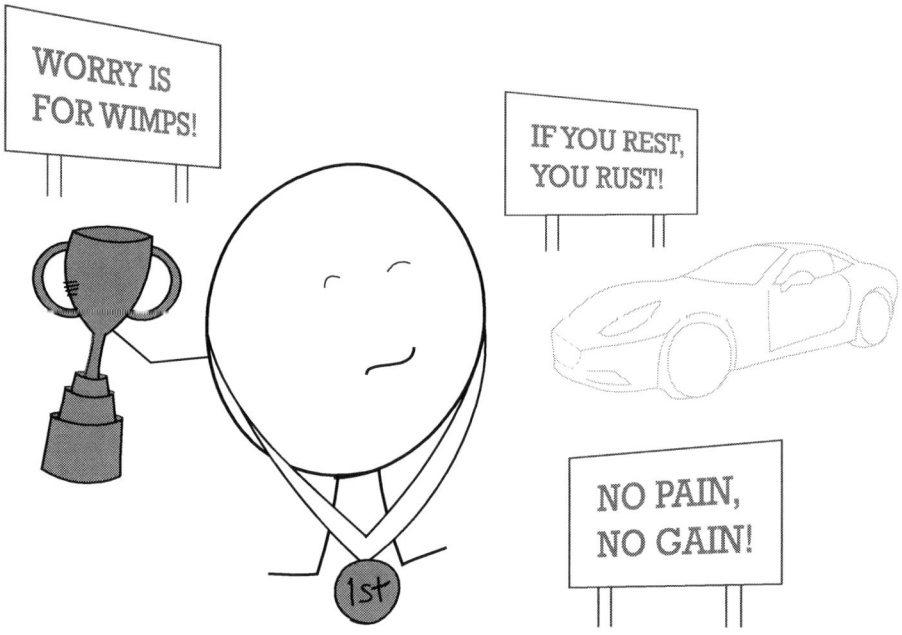

On a good day!

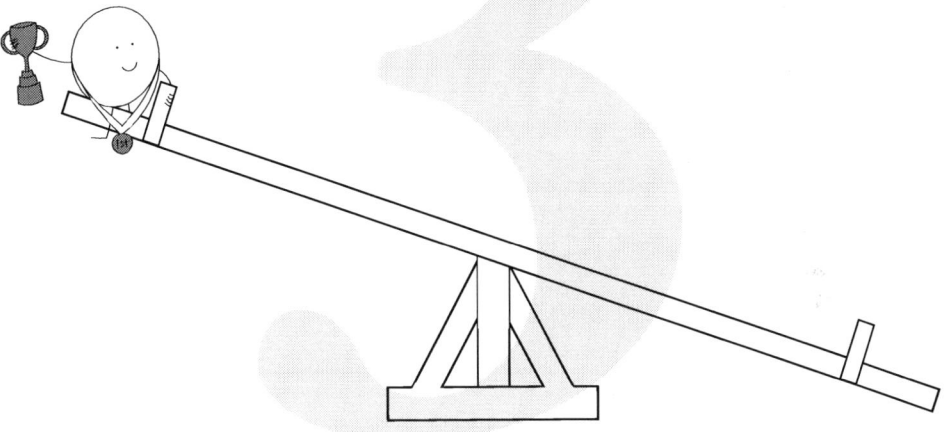

"3s are great to work with - they get things done! If you're in a team with a 3 then there's a good chance you're on the winning team."

3s' networking skills are second to none, their natural charm and their focus on building an image of effusive confidence in their own abilities makes them natural actors and salespeople - they are perfectly suited to the world of marketing, events management and advertising.

"I've teamed up with a 3 who has a real entrepreneurial quality - able to spot opportunities, and always looking for ways to get ahead."

The continuous energy of the heart centre creates in 3s a highly industrious nature, very task driven, producing awesome efficiency; they are supreme achievers... They want to be seen bringing the trophy home.

"... clever 3s know they can't do it all by themselves and so surround themselves with those who can help. If you're on a team with a 3 you must be valuable because 3s wouldn't put up with anyone below par."

On a bad day!

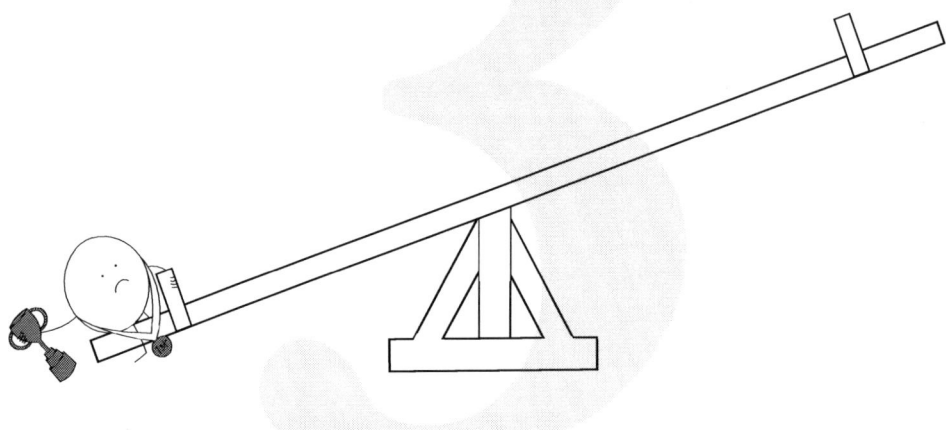

Whilst for some types the trophy might be all about celebrating team achievement or a sense of private satisfaction, the core drive of the 3 craves personal accolades and acknowledgement. An emotionally unhealthy 3 becomes self aggrandising, breathtakingly boastful, over playing genuine success to the point of blatant fabrication. They can be scant in praise, or overtly dismissive, they can use people as a means to an end: overflowing with charm one instant, cold disconnection in the next.

"... (3s) may also look down on people who don't seem to know what they want or where they're heading. The competitive streak in a 3 means there's almost no satisfaction in beating a loser... If you're passive or lack drive then maybe you're not worth dealing with."

"In later years the phrase I hear myself repeat constantly to the point of self-loathing is, 'Do you know what I mean?' – always seeking the affirmation of others."

"...we put ourselves under great pressure to have things looking good and at times this can be ... at the expense of the feelings of others. For example, when we were selling our house some years ago I could see the importance of selling the lifestyle so I had the bread baking in the oven, the coffee percolating, the house pristine, the children shipped out, even if that meant they were sitting at the bottom of the road in the car with their dad in the pouring rain!!! The effort was exhausting but the outcome – instantly successful!"

The insecure need for recognition can result in reluctance to give it to others or even the taking of credit for others' accomplishments. Ruthlessly competitive, they will deceive to achieve.

"I can be quite pretentious at times which can lead to me being both vain and shallow. If a situation is proving difficult, a devious streak can sometimes emerge."

"I am an untidy person but that's no good if you are a 3 as first impressions are vital. So I live in a home that, for the most part, appears modern, funky and stylish, however: open the nearest wardrobe, cupboard or drawer and it will be crammed with a spectacular mess. I have often wondered why I operate like this and can only surmise that there is little gain for a 3 spending hours tidying behind the scenes as who will ever see it?"

Self promotion drives them; they are unable to miss an opportunity to impress: name dropping, chasing success by association either with designer labels and the usual trappings, or sometimes with more unexpected signs of accomplishment.

Focus on the superficial image they are trying to create can make 3s appear and even feel, shallow; they feel like frauds in their desperation to attract respect.

"When not in a healthy space, 3s can get too caught up on the goal and forget to enjoy the journey – taking pleasure in the experience not just getting the result or getting it done. They may also lack ... empathy – so when working with 3s you may find they don't put themselves in other people's shoes."

"I had no idea what kind of a mother I would be as I was never particularly maternal as a youngster, however, with the birth of my first child, my 3 spirit was unleashed: I would be the best mother ever and if that meant 24 hour contact with my boys then so be it. The sacrifices were huge in pursuit of successful motherhood: ...If I was going to do this I was going to do the best job I could."

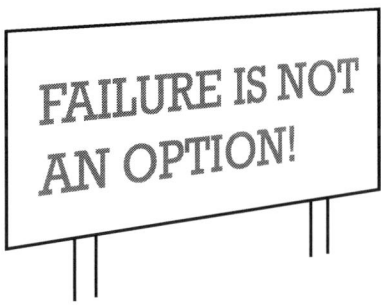

FAILURE IS NOT AN OPTION!

WHO SAYS IT'S ALL ABOUT TAKING PART?!

Underneath this veneer, however, lies a heart type who loves deeply and sincerely, but may struggle to access it or demonstrate it to others. Once convinced of their intrinsic value and reassured of love, they shine. Dynamic and powerful, playful and sharp witted, a healthy 3 drives change, inspiring action in others, leading by focused determination and steady self belief.

"On a good day, he rallies the troops, makes a plan, sees the goal and doesn't get distracted from it. He is so passionate about succeeding, you're inspired to join him."

The peacock is the epitome of the 3:
Fabulously ostentatious, stunning; a bird dressed to impress, the peacock is irresistibly attractive because of its appearance.

Core values for the 3 are likely to include:
success, achievement, efficiency and acknowledgement.

Dazzlingly self assured, they dare us to believe that we too can achieve.

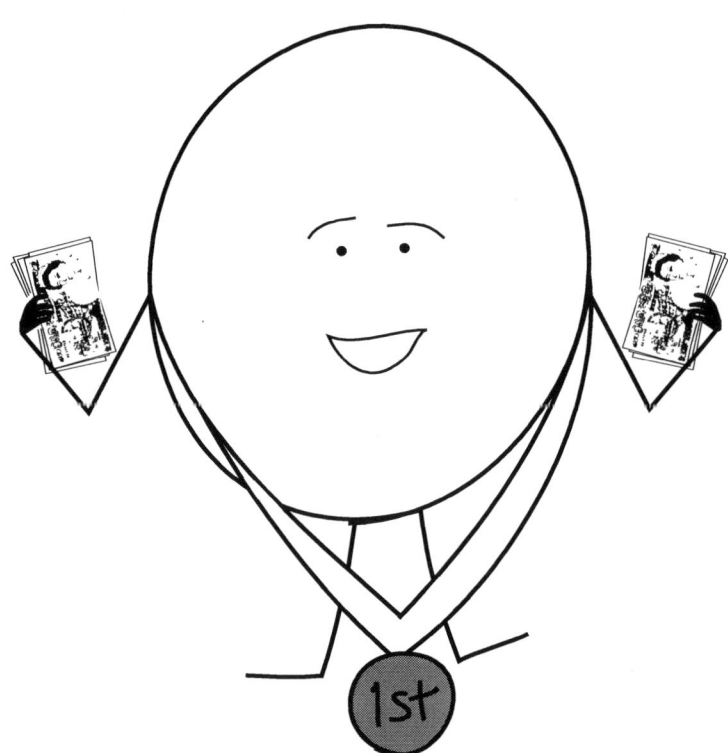

Coaching technique: The wheel of life

The wheel of life is an excellent exercise for anyone to assess how balanced life is at any point in time. It is particularly useful for 3s as, when out of balance, they will invariably become intensely driven 'workaholics'. 1s and 9s will also benefit specifically: 1s may tend towards over work in their desire to be 'good enough' and 9s may lack focus and direction in their need to keep the peace.

Try the following exercise and see how balanced your life is at the moment. It is an excellent exercise to revisit to redress inevitable shifting imbalances in life.

The wheel of life

Here is an example of a 'wheel of life' split into the general areas that make up a life. Your life may contain different areas or have more. Each section needs to be graded in terms of satisfaction, on a scale of one to ten.

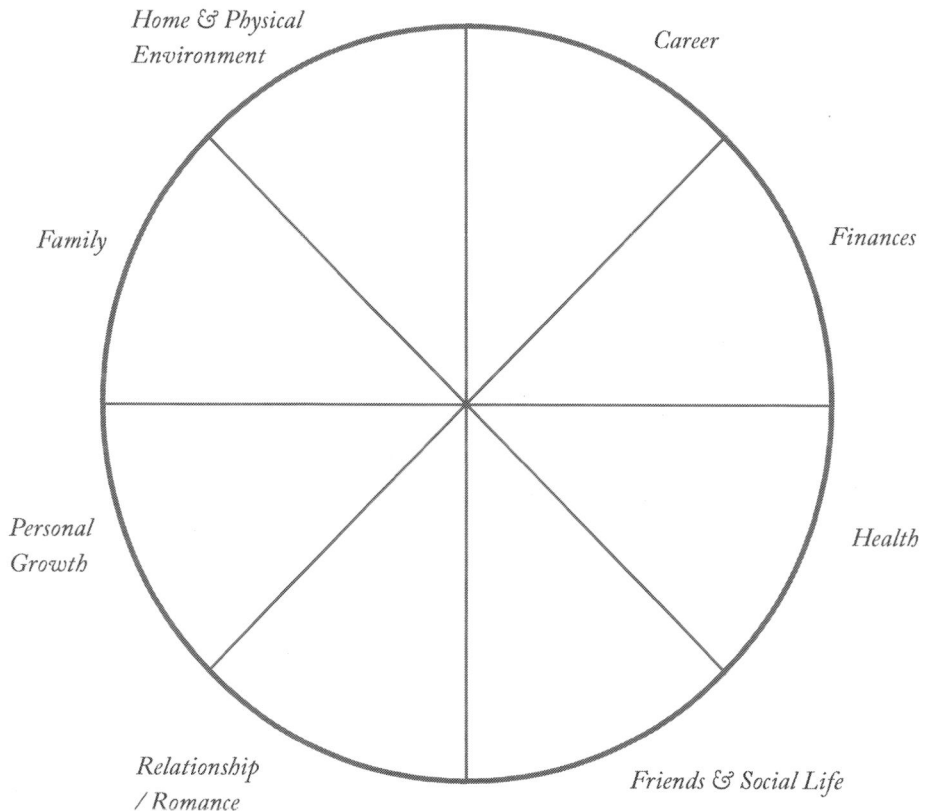

Draw out your own wheel and the areas that make up your own life. Now without too much thought, grade each area on a level of satisfaction between one and ten, using the number that first pops into your head.

The eight sections in the wheel of life represent balance. Regarding the centre of the wheel as 0 and the outer edge as 10, rank your level of satisfaction with each life area by drawing a straight or curved line to create a new outer edge (see example below).
The new perimeter of the circle represents your wheel of life. How bumpy would the ride be if this represented your wheel of life?
This will give you an idea of where the imbalances are in your life, and help you prioritise issues that need resolving.

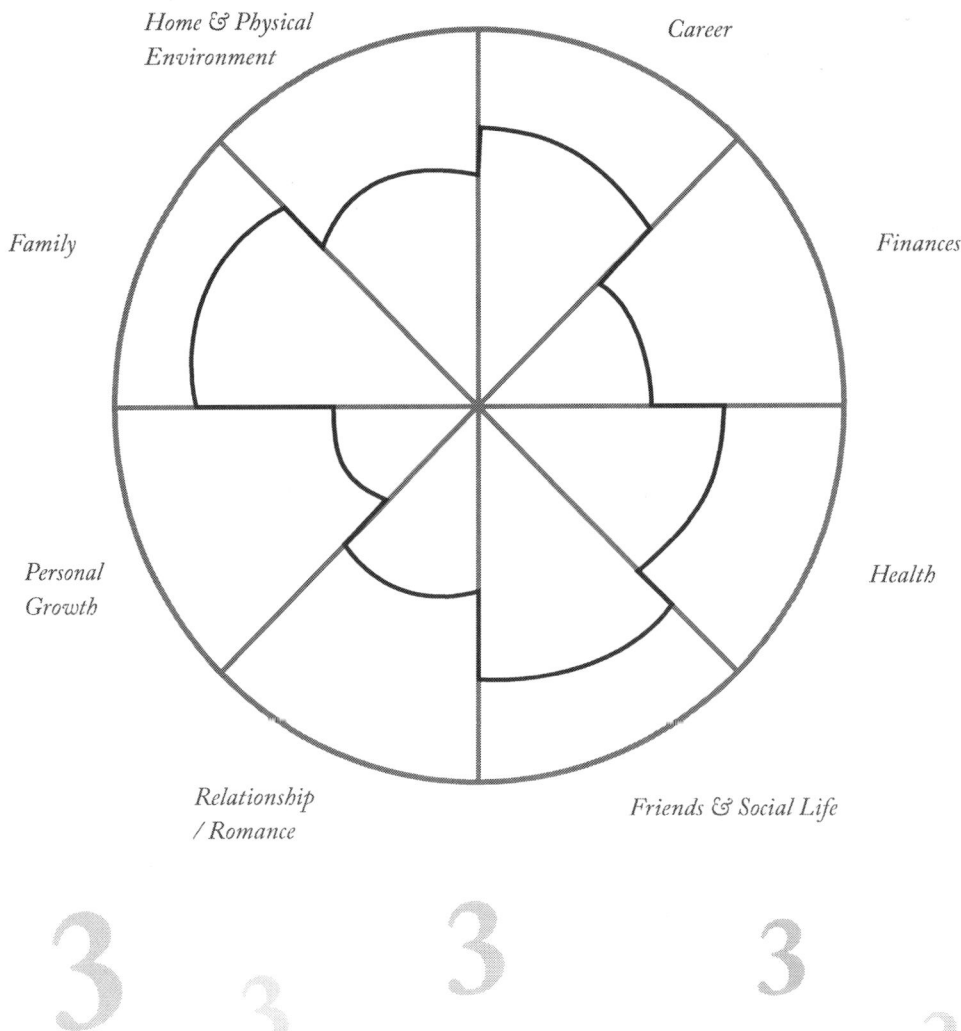

REFLECTION

What has this exercise revealed to you?

What actions could you take to redress the balance of your life?

Do by date: when might you do this?

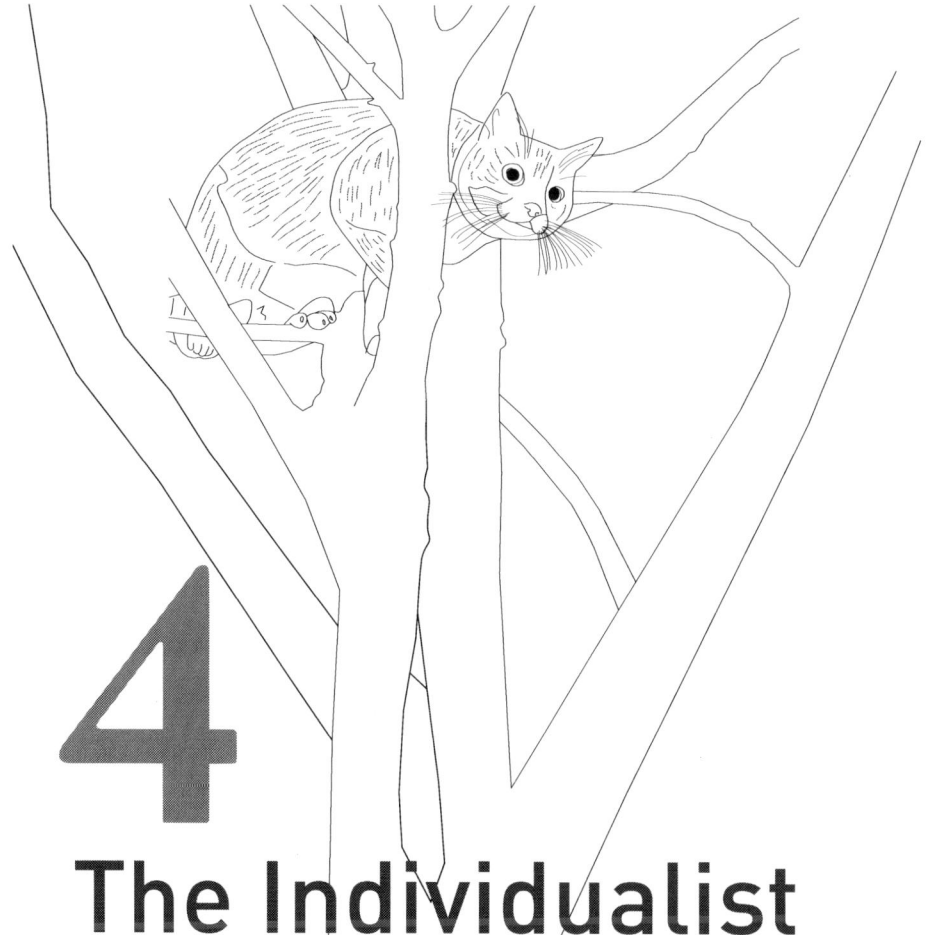

4
The Individualist

"If there's any message to my work, it is ultimately that it's okay to be different, that it's good to be different, that we should question ourselves before we pass judgment on someone who looks different, behaves different, talks different, is a different colour."

Johnny Depp, American actor, film producer, musician

Unique, sensitive, free thinking innovators, 4s are brave and emotionally honest, feeling life's extremes fully and embracing the rich, dramatic tapestry of life in their desire to be authentic – and loved.

"Life generally is very exciting. Anything is possible. With luck on my side, the best possible outcome is definitely achievable. There is always a positive solution to problems, people will want to be honourable and good will prevail."

4s are the last of the heart types, seeking love, not by serving like the 2 or impressing like the 3 but by being different or special, needing others' attention or help.
Core values for a 4 are likely to include: individuality, creativity, integrity and beauty.

"Being a 4 in balance allows me to do things in my quirky, individualistic way."

4s' emotional range allows them to translate the whole of the human experience in emotional terms from agony to ecstasy. They are creative, artistic expressers of the profound beauty and fragility of their life's story: the tragic poets, dramatic songwriters, impassioned artists all convey truth through emotive means – they 'wear their heart on their sleeve'.

"... being a 4 is exhausting! The range of emotions I experience regularly is large and the impact of them intense. The range of emotions I experience is also exhilarating and I don't think I could live without them."

On a good day!

Emotionally balanced 4s are warm and empathic, their ability to feel the intensity of others' pain gives them a huge capacity for compassion; they can be massively supportive to those in distress. 4s feel instantly the full ramifications of a situation – they will understand impact and potential fallout for all. Just as the 8 champions the cause of the vulnerable or the underdog, 4s are the emotional spokesperson for those with no voice: they demand that we listen and feel for them too.

"(4s) ... will go out of their way to help someone in genuine distress"

"On form I am caring about others and will deliver even quite difficult messages in a way that combines sensitivity and humour."

4s have to be true to the whole of who they are: the heart centre's search for love generates in 4s an emotional integrity which drives them to deliver the painful truth no matter what the cost – the classic 'prophet in the wilderness'. 4s are determined to face and embrace pain; they have an innate awareness of the downside, troubleshooting potential problems in any given situation. 4s are vital to the planning of any operation as they will unerringly spot where the whole project will fail, so attuned are they to the emotional fabric underpinning any endeavour. Whilst 9s have an instinct for misalignment, forensic 5s' expertise will show up shortcomings in others' thinking and 6s have an intuitive 'knowing' that something isn't going to work; 4s have a subconscious **need** to find a flaw, to be uncomfortable with what others buy into, to be the one voice of dissent.

On a bad day!

"......I have a sense of foreboding that the adventures of life are coming to an end... feeling intense disappointment ... at times I feel complete shame..."

Aptly named 'the irritant', 4s when out of balance, can be difficult to be around. Their core drive for attention creates a need to feel the emotional pain of life: their sensitivity and readiness to feel upset makes unhealthy 4s unpopular in groups as there is an expectation that they will feel bad and that their feelings will be expressed destructively, with or without words.

"I am a difficult character, I can be over sensitive, moody, gloomy, 'dark' (perhaps this is why I love horror stories and dramatic tragedy best) and when I'm in the grip of a 'bad mood' life goes on hold, jobs don't get done and communications with other people are poor."

4s can become so engulfed in feeling the flaws in every situation that pain can become all consuming – suffering becomes almost an end in itself – rather than troubleshooting and moving to solutions, 4s can descend into the abyss, seduced by the need to fully feel the bleakest of human emotion. Feeling flawed, sometimes only subconsciously, 4s create cycles of rejection and dependency, leaving trails of destruction – broken friendships, tortured romances, family feuds, unfinished projects: all further evidence of the depths of their afflictions. These will be deeply felt internally, they send ripples of discomfort to others, messages of distress to which they hope others will respond. They envy others who seem to have what they lack.

"When out of balance I can be very easily hurt and this leads to strong feelings of injustice. At these times I can be enveloped in my own thoughts. I am very rigid ... (unable)... to see things in a balanced way. Waves of resentment and anger flood over me and my withdrawal from others is in very dramatic contrast to my balanced self."

Caught in a vortex of powerful negative emotion, the 4s' need for love and attention drives lamenting and woefulness: unhealthy 4s turn every situation into a self-obsessed drama in which truth can become distorted and they are inevitably the victim. This can drive away the very attention they crave, leaving 4s feeling ever more alone with their misery. Whilst 2s can become overtly needy, even hysterical in their quest for appreciation, dramatising their self sacrifice to attract attention, 4s tend to dramatise their pain: when out of balance they suffer from an insatiable desire for sympathy.

4s seek acknowledgement that they are feeling a depth of pain others will not allow themselves to experience and therefore cannot fully understand.

"The depression is a black hole into which everything is sucked. I feel misunderstood and judged when people try to chivvy me out of my black hole and woe betide anyone who tells me 'It's not as bad as all that!'. It absolutely IS! I have their card marked as a traitor."

"... I'm not being self indulgent or shirking responsibility when I'm in this state of mind, I'm doing a lot of work on myself in this dark and morbid place and it is important to feel the pain fully and face the fears. ... I don't want to be chivvied I want to be allowed (even though I know this means I'm being unreasonably miserable and unpleasant to live with) to go down to the bottom of the emotional pit of despair!"

When assured that their value is known, their truths welcomed, the gentleness and warmth of the 4 can be transformational.

They have a gift to offer: when out of balance they may not wrap it well, but when feeling loved, free to bring their truth to the table without sacrificing personal integrity, they bring poignancy and passion to their message. The grit in the oyster becomes the unique beauty of the pearl.

"I have very strong political beliefs and social values which have driven my decision making processes over the years. A strong belief is that service to others is noble and that teaching is a service."

"I have a very active imagination and I can make it offer me new visions of how life could be… This gives me the freedom to respond honestly whilst constantly gauging how things are received and moving quickly, keeping the main objective in my sight – but involving others in reaching the same conclusion."

The black cat is the epitome of the 4:
Enigmatic, independent and aloof at times, seeking attention and love on their own terms, cats epitomize beauty, style and elegance.

Core values for the 4 are likely to include:
individuality, creativity, integrity and beauty.

The courage and intensity of the 4s' ability to connect with human emotion touches our hearts at the deepest level, compelling us to mobilize, lifting the human spirit to new heights of compassion and love.

Coaching technique: Positive affirmations

4s and also 6s can struggle with looking at the positives in life; 4s can become overwhelmed by pain and drama, which keeps them stuck in low moods and can prevent them from moving towards something better. The use of affirmations may be quite a challenge for 4s, but can offer them the lift they need to break free of negative cycles, building a positive platform from which to experience life. Scientific studies of the reticular activating system in the brain, show that what we focus our attention on is what the brain attunes to and will selectively notice, thereby increasing the frequency of thoughts and experiences to match.

This exercise is designed to create different thoughts and make them the habitual focus for the mind. All types will benefit from the boost this exercise will give, when used regularly. They can also support forward focus and goal setting. Positive affirmations are strong, positive statements which focus you on what you want to achieve. Positive affirmations help to drown out those mental, discouraging gremlins we all experience and help to boost confidence. Many people repeat affirmations every morning & evening, but they must be followed up with action to take things forward.

Keep to the **three 'P's**: Make them:

Positive: avoid negative phrasing - say what you want, not what you don't want.
Present tense: your subconscious mind takes things literally.
Personal: be as specific as you can with what makes these statements important for YOU.

Use your new positive thoughts (e.g." I am calm & relaxed" "I am a confident person" "I can do this") repeatedly - by continually repeating them to yourself, you can influence your subconscious mind and begin to alter limiting beliefs that may have held you back in the past. Repetition is the key.

Write your affirmations down and read them several times during the day (at least a dozen repetitions once in the morning and once at night would be advisable). At first you may feel foolish. Negative thoughts may come up to start with, but you need to persevere. Positive affirmations must be said for a minimum of 21 days for it to become habit forming. Don't give up if you do not see and feel results within a couple of days (although you may certainly start to feel more positive about the particular issue); stick with your affirmations for at least a month.

Working with a group of disabled young people resulted in a particularly inspirational list of affirmations which included:

I am happy.
I am confident.
I am calm and relaxed.
I am funny.
I am creative.
I like myself.
I am helpful.
I am beautiful.
I am in control.
I am at peace.

My life is rich and fulfilling.
I am a sexy guy.
I am a positive role model.
I am achieving my goals.
I am healthy and fit.
I have a kind heart.
I am centred and balanced.
I can achieve anything.
Life is beautiful.

These may inspire your own list of affirmations.

REFLECTION

What affirmations would you choose?

What has doing this exercise revealed to you?

If you chose to, how could you build affirmations into your daily/weekly routines?

Do by date: when might you do this?

The Forensic 5

*"Be nice to nerds.
Chances are you'll end up working for one."*

Bill Gates, American business magnate, philanthropist, investor, computer programmer, and inventor

Reflective, self sufficient loners, 5s are objective and perceptive, single minded in their quest for knowledge, they want their own space to acquire and assimilate information.

'Leave me in my cardboard box with my books and I am at my happiest.'

5s are the first of the head types, seeking safety by gathering facts: the more they know, the safer they feel. 5s are the most obvious of the head types, they are the classic logical thinkers, nose always in a book, specialists in their chosen fields; this is the realm of the genius. Core values are likely to include: learning, knowledge, safety and independence.

"Breathtakingly incisive, she is a true genius, a researcher to the core. She is immensely challenging, she drives innovation and change."

The brilliance of a 5 can be multifaceted. Whatever healthy 5s pursue, true expertise will generally emerge from their relentless research, whether it be academic learning, innovation, scientific and artistic exploration or the mechanics of anything, including money making. Highly functioning 5s are wise, curious and highly insightful. Often seen as the eccentric professor, the stereotypical 'geek' or 'nerd'; with the recent technological explosion, the niche of the 5 now brings greater status and respect than ever before. 5s have an objectivity and detachment: the medical consultant, for example, even in the most traumatic of circumstances, functions logically and calmly without emotion.

"In balance my husband who is... a great combination of a kind and tender human being... has that highly logical and step by step approach to life."

On a good day!

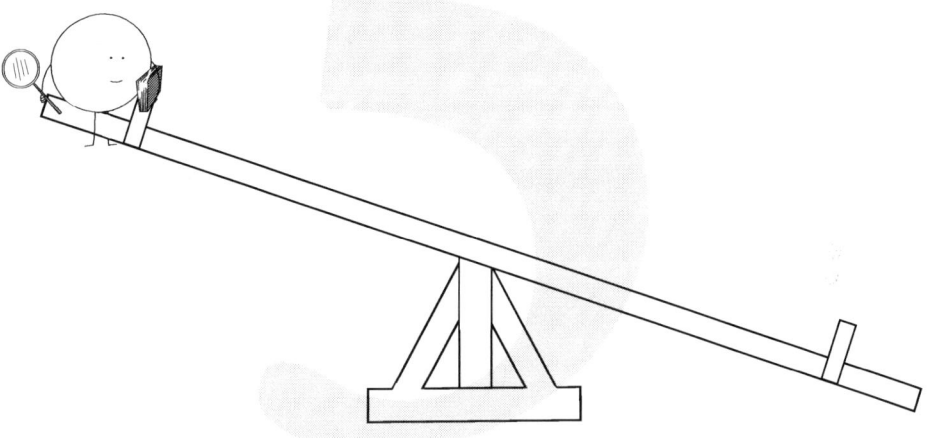

The 5s' self sufficiency creates a sharp contrast to the heart centre types; there is no 'neediness' about them - in fact they overtly crave distance and privacy. A 5's house is not so much a castle as a fortress. When they do lower the drawbridge, they can be uncommonly tender, although moments of intimacy are closely guarded: they fear exposure and will do anything to avoid overdone displays of excessive emotion.

At a funeral, a 5 commented to his wife:

"I don't know why everyone is so upset - it's just a process we all go through, living and dying, no surprises."

"I am not very good at explaining my perspective … putting me in a room for a long period with one person is only going to elicit a stressed response however nice they are because it is an extension of socializing."

"I have always felt very pressurized by the social people around me who think there is something wrong with me or them if I don't want to join in. I remember being invited to a party as a child and crying at the very thought of having to go. My feelings have not changed with time and the phrase 'You'll love it once you are there,' is simply not true. (I do know I was sent to parties with the best of intentions!)"

On a bad day!

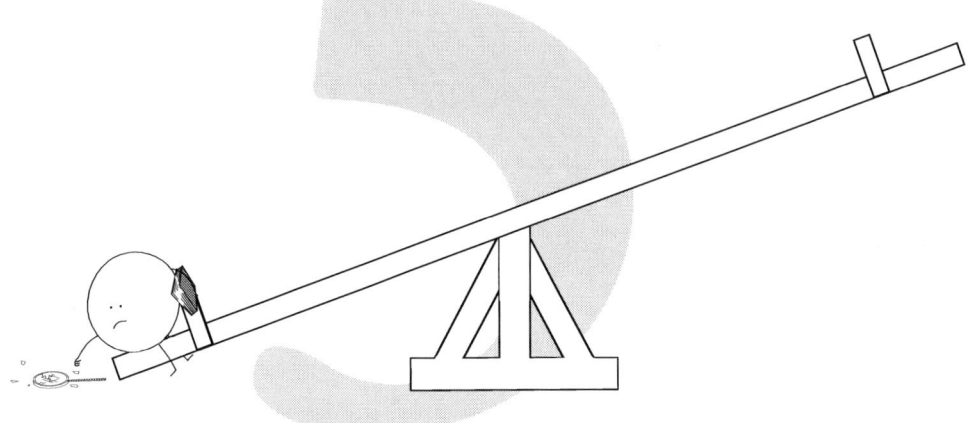

When out of balance this fear of emotion creates a fierce isolation: the 5 becomes reclusive, driving others away, either physically, by living or working alone, or emotionally. Sneering and sarcastic, they can be aggressively critical. Their razor-sharp objectivity becomes harsh and even cruel, their surgical comments deliver brutal truths without feeling.

"Out of kilter, his stubbornness and view that only he is right, coupled with strong criticism of others can be incredibly destructive. Any patience or insight into how others are perceiving the situation goes out the window."

Protecting their own vulnerability leads to a survivalist mentality: 5s will hoard - information and things - with a 'just in case', 'packrat' instinct. Out of balance 5s can be stingy and miserly, in their drive to feel safe. The quest for cerebral strength leads to a neglect of the body - unhealthy 5s can forget to clean or eat and the basic, social fundamentals are utterly obscure to them.

"His garage would barely open, crammed as it is with old paint pots, bikes from 30 years ago, all things mechanical, garden tools and anything that might be of use one day in the future. It was a treasure trove of oddities."

5s use knowledge to counter their core sense of vulnerability. Guarding against inner overwhelm, 5s may perceive unexpected or impromptu attempts to connect as threatening and will tend to rebuff these, sometimes to the point of rudeness. They can appear arrogant and dismissive, putting others down and being scant in praise: behaviours seen in 3s, but far from seeking attention, the driver for the 3, the 5 is seeking safety. Whilst 3s court applause, 5s dread exposure and are often socially awkward or shy.

"I am very close to my siblings but not in a demonstrative way… I don't like the staying over and socializing bit and if I am in one of their houses will probably say less than ten words and feel very stressed and try to find something practical to occupy my time."

"I still go to all the normal family things and make a passable attempt at looking happy…"

Profound gentleness may come as a surprise from a 5, but it is at the core of this brilliant, fear driven type, shown only when they feel completely safe. Their wise, pragmatic objectivity ensures that practical solutions prevail.

"The other funny thing is that I am very demonstrative with my kids – my own parents and siblings often comment on it because I am so undemonstrative with everyone else."

"…she will often contact me when I least expect it (and most need it), offering a support and a reassurance that takes my breath away with its warmth and reassurance. Always with no fuss, minimal wordage, she can't bear being 'fluffy'!"

The owl is the epitome of the 5:
Solitary, wise, aloof and yet astute, the owl represents knowledge and learning.

Core values for the 5 are likely to include:
learning, knowledge, safety and independence.

True innovators on the leading edge of discovery, they create by pushing the boundaries of the unknown; they challenge us to do likewise.

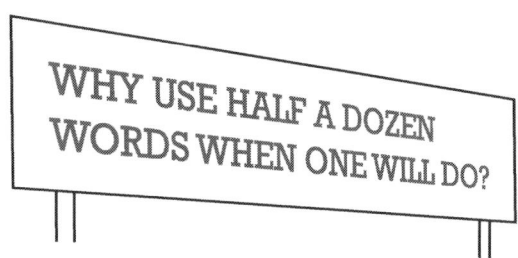

Coaching technique: The anchoring exercise

This is a very simple, yet highly effective exercise for connecting with and making the most of our good feeling emotions. As 5s will tend to avoid emotional awareness, anchoring is ideal for this personality type, although all types can benefit from it.

Think of Pavlov's dog. Every time Pavlov's dog was given food, a bell was rung. The dog subconsciously associated the sound of the bell with food until eventually just the sound of the bell made the dog salivate. Pavlov's dog subconsciously associated the sound of the bell with food. The same thing happens with humans. How do you feel when you hear the sound of the dentist's drill? Tense and uncomfortable? We associate the sound of the dentist's drill with pain and tension.

There are positive anchors too. When you see sports men and women clenching their fists and shouting "Yes!" to pump themselves up, it's because it makes them feel confident and energetic.

You have probably experienced listening to the radio, for example, when a particular song is played which reminds you of a happy time: a fantastic holiday, an old flame, your childhood – and you found all the feelings associated with that time came flooding back.

Often we are unaware of our anchors and how they affect us: but we may notice that the smell of freshly cut grass or fresh coffee can perk us up and make us mentally alert.

With this anchoring technique, you can create your own anchors to produce specific emotions when you most need them.

All you need to do is:

Remember a time when you felt that emotion and then in the peak of the emotion as you are remembering it, do something unusual - pinch your ear, tweak your nose, squeeze your wrist. It doesn't matter what you do so long as it is specific and not something you do every day.

It can take time to practise visualizing a past experience and remembering a specific memory and **you must be at the peak of the emotion before you create the anchor,** but if you persevere, it really does work.

As an example, for this exercise, let's take the ability to feel relaxed. The physical anchor we will create will be: squeezing your finger and thumb together.
This exercise will enable you to trigger that feeling of relaxation, whenever you want.

Read through the instructions. If you wish, (although this is not necessary) you can record them for yourself to play back with your eyes closed, or ask a friend to read them to you.

Sit comfortably on your chair. Close your eyes. Uncross your arms and legs as this can cause physical tension.
Put one hand on your stomach above the navel and feel yourself breathing in and out, in and out. Relax your hands and place them in your lap.

Unclench your teeth, drop your shoulders creating space between your shoulder and ears. Unclench your fists.
Be aware of the position of your body on the chair.

Concentrate on your head, your shoulders and neck, your upper body, your stomach and your breathing, your posture, your lower body and your legs and feet.
Listen to your breathing for about ten breaths… do not change your breathing
- just listen to it.

Now take slightly deeper breaths, breathing into your stomach and as you breathe out, breathe out of your stomach.

Breathe slowly in…and out…in…and out….in and out.

Think back to all the many times when you have felt calm and relaxed. Then focus on the time when you felt most calm and relaxed, when you felt particularly calm and relaxed. If you can't think of a time, imagine. It doesn't matter where you were or what you were doing. Think of it as clearly as you can.

Reflect on the answers to the following questions and try to re-experience that memory. Let the feelings of calm and relaxation increase.

What were you saying?
What were you doing?
How were you breathing?
What was your posture like?
How was your body language?
What was your facial expression?
How did you feel?

Try to remember everything.

Close your eyes, make it as strong as possible and then squeeze your index finger and thumb together (your anchor).

Go through the procedure 10 times, using your anchor at the end of each visualization. You have now created a relaxing anchor. Activate your anchor.

You should feel a sense of calm and relaxation. You have just helped your subconscious associate calm and relaxation with a squeezed thumb and finger.

REFLECTION

What has this exercise revealed to you?

What actions could you take to make the most of this exercise and raise your emotional self awareness?

How will you make sure you take these actions when they are most needed?

The Teammate

"Without a team you can achieve nothing. It's a team that wins a tournament, and not an individual player."

"I am the same person as always and I have the good fortune to play in a great team. It was an historic year for Barca and for me but it's thanks to the work of everyone."

Lionel Messi, Argentinian footballer, after being named Fifa World Footballer of the Year

Loyal, dependable team-players, 6s are efficient and ordered, busy organising life, internally and/or externally, to keep themselves and others safe.

"I like being structured and organised because I hate wasting time, I feel that I am reliable and dedicated and always try my best to please, and do not fritter away my true friendships."

6s are the second of the head centre types, seeking safety through their attempts to make life predictable. Whilst 5s build fortresses of knowledge, 6s search for systems and hierarchical structures to give them a sense of security. Core values for a 6 are likely to include: trust, loyalty, teamwork and reliability.

"I need ... (someone) to go to if there are problems and decisions to be made."

Healthy 6s are conscientious, hardworking, community orientated and highly responsible, without the need for praise. Humble and unassuming, they elevate the contribution of others. They intuit the needs of the 'team' - be it family or organisation, they have a 'sixth sense' for signs of unrest or potential trouble ahead, checking and questioning everything to preempt danger. Risk averse, they are natural health and safety experts; 6s give their all for the wellbeing of the whole, preserving and protecting their own.

"The 6s in my life are not afraid to tell me what they think and are not averse to speaking their mind, generally it's their need to keep me safe because they care about me.
Being told that my long awaited, day-old, new convertible car could be dangerous in a crash is a good example of this need to keep me safe even if it rained on my parade."

On a good day!

THE WHOLE IS GREATER THAN THE SUM OF THE PARTS

Naturally cautious and careful, the courage of the 6 is sudden and often surprising. Apparently the least likely to take a risk, they will act with lightning speed and certainty when threatened. Unexpected heroes, their strength is understated and hidden - they take control in order to protect, not to acquire power.

"(My) ... friend ... is not always good at fighting her own corner ... However, she refers to herself as the Rottweiler where her family and friends are concerned. She is fiercely protective of those she feels loyal to and will go into battle for anyone she cares about."

"I will speak my mind if I feel wronged or if someone I love is wronged even if it means falling out with someone. If someone hurts me, I can't forgive them and I will never forget."

Trust is paramount to a 6. Even the healthiest 6 needs distance initially to weigh up risks when meeting a new person or situation. Checking, challenging, to the point of cynicism - these are inbuilt safety mechanisms for 6s who will not give their trust until they are sure it will not be abused. Yet when they do trust in a concept or person, the sceptic becomes the convert and they are 'in' hook line and sinker, they love nothing better than to give themselves wholeheartedly to a cause in which they can trust - and feel safe.

"...6s ... take a while to decide to trust someone and do not open themselves up to new people until they feel safe to do so. Once you are in their circle they are fiercely loyal..."

On a bad day!

The nervous energy of the head centre is more evident in 6s than in the other head types: their drive for safety can make them edgy and sharp when insecure. Wary 6s will test loyalty continuously, reading body language, picking up on signs and signals, on the alert for mixed messages, which are an anathema to the 6. Quite the opposite of the 5s with their lack of connection with the body and its emotional messages, 6s are likely to be super-aware, to the point of paranoia when security is undermined.

".. I can have problems with self confidence and self doubt. I can be defensive, anxious and suspicious of people."

6s are born worriers, anxiety is their default position: it creates tension in and around their bodies, alertness in their eyes. It is palpable from a distance when a 6 is on edge – very much the 'cat on a hot tin roof', ready to leap or to strike, if necessary. For insecure 6s this becomes a fear which spreads like wildfire to all aspects of life; they become hyper-vigilant, envisaging worst-case scenarios and becoming suspicious of events and intentions. Phobic behaviour can emerge, limiting 6s to a decreasing circle of safety as they dread catastrophe and expect calamity. Stubborn complaining and procrastination often accompanies ever more obsessive attempts to control their environment or people; 6s can become fixated on hygiene, tidiness and/or security measures, checking and re-checking that they are safe.

"I can't abide untidiness, mess or chaos... My house and life have to be 'ship shape' or I won't be able to relax" "...I can't leave a job half way through – it has to be finished..."

"... He won't do a DIY job without switching the electricity off at the main power station... he hides his car keys for a weekend away... Another friend can't face a Friday morning without bleaching the whole house..."

"I can be very cautious and will foresee problems... I feel the fear of what could happen always holds me back. I need support from others to keep me feeling secure and in control."

6s can become brittle and rigid in their fearful need to compartmentalize life, to keep everything in its place: scheming, manipulating people and events as if playing chess. There is a covertness about the 6: 3s scheme to take the glory, 1s trust few to avoid criticism, but 6s need their systems and structures safe – they fear disintegration. They need conformity, order: change is a threat, deviance an abhorrence. Unhealthy 6s will drive logic to extremes, they follow the letter of the law with disregard for its spirit; they become the creators of red tape and crippling bureaucracy. Full of contradictions, 6s love hierarchy but may be the very ones to flout it after years of loyalty if their trust is broken. 6s generally avoid public attention, but may attract a spotlight with an outburst of sudden confidence, when safe, or anger when threatened. They crave rules, but some want to know them… and then delight in breaking them.

"I am a belt and braces person."

"I don't always understand myself as I can be fearful and also brave, I can be very strong and decisive and then I can't make a decision."

Supremely stealthy, natural spies, 6s can blend in when they need to – completely 'disappearing' to keep themselves safe: people-watching is a compulsion. When sure of themselves and the people around them, the wonderfully impish, playful essence of the 6 bursts forth. When secure, they are frank, open and utterly unguarded – their trust is absolute.

The meerkat is the epitome of the 6:
Ever watchful, uncannily attuned to each other and the group, their colonies thrive on their highly organised, collective, altruistic approach to safeguarding their own.

Core values for the 6 are likely to include:
trust, loyalty, teamwork and reliability.

Ultimate team players, 6s show us the strength in pulling together; they call us to stand shoulder to shoulder, harnessing the power of the group.

Coaching technique: The worry chart

Many people worry. 6s when out of balance, will expend immense amounts of energy worrying about anything and everything. 1s also spend a lot of time worrying, but whilst 6s worry about safety and trust, 1s tend to worry about whether they have done the right thing or whether or not they will be judged to be good enough.
By writing down worries, they are removed from the mind and placed onto paper, an empowering act which in itself can put situations into perspective and reduce the feeling of overwhelm.
For anyone finding themselves worried or anxious, the following exercise is a powerful tool for returning to a calmer state of mind.

Start by sorting your worries into the following possible categories:

1) Important events that have happened

2) Important events that could happen

3) Unimportant events

4) Areas for genuine concern

For each worry or concern, try to articulate what aspect of it is worrying or concerning you - take time to word this in one clear and concise sentence.
Consider what you might be really afraid of and how realistic your worry actually is. On a scale of 1-10, how significant is this worry? How important will this worry be in 6 months' time?

Consider the damage that worrying is doing to your state of mind, the impact on your body and to your experience of life at this time.
How would life change if you could let go of this fear and worry?
What could you learn from this?
What steps could you take to remove or at least reduce this worry?

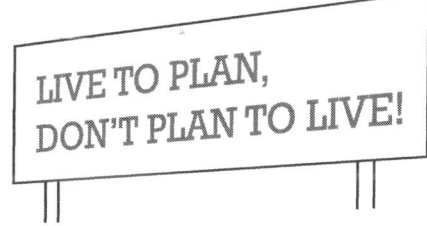

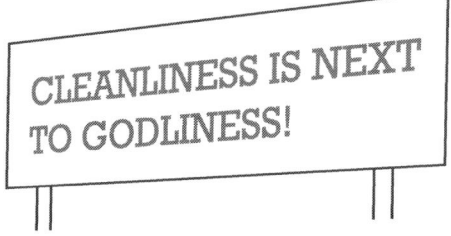

The worry chart

Important events that have happened:

Important events that could happen:

Unimportant events:

Areas for genuine concern:

What action will I take?

How, specifically, will I ensure the action is completed?

When will I complete this?

REFLECTION

What has this exercise revealed to you?

What actions could you take as a result of your learning, to make use of it next time worrying becomes an issue for you?

How will you remind yourself to do this?

7 The Adventurer

"A business has to be involving, it has to be fun and it has to exercise your creative instincts."

"My general attitude to life is to enjoy every minute of every day. I never do anything with a feeling of, 'Oh God, I've got to do this today.'"

Sir Richard Branson, English entrepreneur and founder of the 'Virgin' group

Fun-loving, upbeat, natural entertainers, 7s are lively and active, constantly seeking new experiences, fresh territory; they want life to be exciting and engaging.

"I feel full of energy, being my usual bouncy, bubbly self."

7s are the least obvious of the head centre types - they do not appear outwardly fear-based: fear does not limit them, it actually drives them to 'push the envelope' further into more and more extreme experiences. Whilst 5s seek safety through knowledge, 6s through security and structures, 7s seek safety through stimulation thus avoiding boredom - their subconscious fears stillness. Core values for a 7 are likely to include: fun, excitement, creativity, innovation.

"She is an optimist; she has an innate joy of life and brings to life any room she should step into."

When flourishing, 7s are outgoing, risk taking entrepreneurs, pioneering and innovative. Disinterested in irrelevant opinions, seeking the thrill of stimulation, they have a boundless desire to blaze new trails – 'Why do something that's been done before?'

"As a child she was always asking, 'What's next? What's next?' even at a theme park, she would be asking what we would be doing later!"

"I am future focused and thrive on goals and ideas."

Multi-talented mavericks: leaping into new projects just for the fun factor makes them bold. They can learn at incredible speed, intuitively picking out the essence of a new skill – confidence filling in any gaps – they will happily make up what they don't actually know.

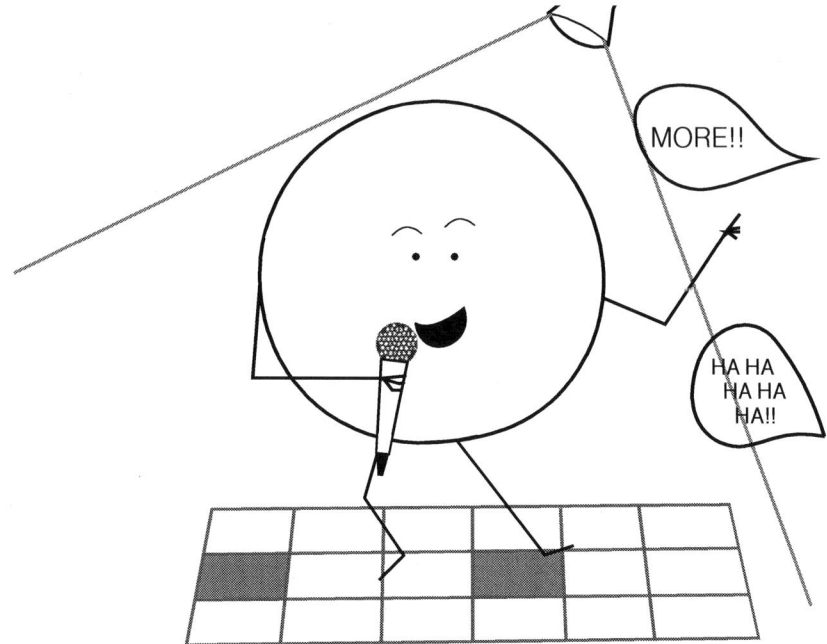

On a good day!

The combination sees them through to stunning success. They surf a wave of supreme expectation that they absolutely can be, do and have what they want. Eternal optimists, embellishing to get the most out of every experience, especially if it will entertain, they appear to lead a 'charmed' existence. Unlike the 3s who do all for the trophies and the accolades, 7s are drawn by the sheer entertainment value of the ride. There is a childlike 'Peter Pan' innocence to their achievements: fabulous raconteurs, they enjoy sharing the tales of their disasters as readily as their successes; the laughter of an audience is irresistible.

"…the life and soul of the party, always upbeat and entertaining… always want to be performing."
"Generally she brightens up my life."

These quirky, 'off the wall', natural comedians are the font of head centre creativity, which fizzes out, in a champagne-bubbling effervescence: their challenge is to channel and direct the gush of ideas.

"… I have a strong imagination and sense of empathy, which means I can generate ideas and be creative, BUT it also means if I ponder or dwell on something negative it can grow out of proportion and become quite consuming. This may be why I don't stop and dwell on things too much."

"The healthy and unhealthy sides of a 7 … can … overlap which makes it difficult to spot when I am crossing over into the 'dark side'… I am excited by variety and change and I am motivated by what I enjoy – all good. But sometimes there is a sense of constant wanting to be moving onto the next thing – not stopping for breath."

On a bad day!

The 'creative fizz' can turn frenetic and frenzied; an addiction to the 'buzz' can drive 7s to ever greater extremes in what becomes a desperate need to satisfy their craving for the next 'high'. This thrill-quest can result in 7s taking serious risks with health, finances, relationships; living 'on the edge' can take a terrible toll.

"My daughter claims she suffers from FOMO a Fear Of Missing Out which makes her life a complete juggling act, trying to fit everything in. She would much rather go without sleep than miss out on anything involving friends or family. Her wardrobe of impulsive buys represents the layout of her own jumbled and erratic mind: she has no concept of a well-ordered capsule wardrobe."

7s, fearful of missing out on anything, juggle impossible numbers of activities, clowning around with the 'dropped balls' but failing to face the damage resulting from the disasters that follow. Unreliability becomes the default for unhealthy 7s, whose thinking can become scattered and chaotic. They will then struggle with commitment, fearing being 'tied down', in case a more interesting option arises – one eye is always on the horizon.

"As a result of not being good at staying still mentally or physically, impatience can arise and frustrate me and those around me. I don't like being held up!"

"When out of balance, I become extremely unfocused and easily distracted. I don't know where to begin with tasks, get lost in something irrelevant, feeling 'away with the fairies'."

7s can avoid facing the mundane deeds of day to day life – procrastination impacts on wellbeing; vitality is sapped into frantic attempts to keep everything afloat. Life dissolves into riotous, last-minute madness. Unhealthy 7s suffer an unquenchable thirst for more – they can become bleak and depressive at the prospect of a life which can never deliver enough, never please enough, never offer enough to satisfy them.

*"By procrastinating I become disorganized, I feel weighed down, my life becomes chaotic. I feel constantly on the go, can't seem to relax, I become irritated and fidgety.
Though frenetically active, I am drained of energy, becoming exhausted, run down and not myself."*

As a 7 discovers the beauty of just 'being', they can focus the pleasures of 'doing'; they need to feel grounded in the deliciousness of pure existence, fully satisfied in the now, before going out to seek more. This nourishment in the now allows their massive creativity to spread and grow – a tree branching out to new experiences, needing to be firmly rooted in the stillness of the earth.

"Meditation is helping me because it allows me to stop, recharge and switch off those frantic thoughts and just be. It's a challenge for me as a 7 to sit still and just breathe, but I find it helps."

The chimp is the epitome of the 7:
Clever and comical, the chimp's antics are irresistible; unexpectedly alert to danger, however, when spooked, animated play bursts instantly into fearful frenzy.

Core values for a 7 are likely to include:
fun, excitement, creativity and innovation.

Inquisitive and playful, these 'Why not?' visionaries dare us to imagine the fun we could have making the impossible possible and they challenge us to 'make it so'.

Coaching technique: Relaxation

As the Adventurer can struggle to be still in both mind and body, the ability to relax fully can be particularly beneficial for this type, although the positive effects of relaxation are universal.

You could ask someone to read this three step relaxation exercise to you, you could record it for yourself on an audio device or just read it through a few times and follow the shape of it in your own way with your eyes closed. The specifics of the words are not important.

Note:
In most circumstances, relaxation is highly beneficial. Occasionally, under certain circumstances, relaxation may create negative effects and therefore the following points should be considered.

• Training in relaxation should never be viewed as a substitute for medical treatment, whenever a disorder is present or suspected.

• Relaxation is not generally recommended for people suffering from hallucinations or other psychotic symptoms, for which imagery is inappropriate.

• Variations in blood pressure may occur in relaxation training, it can rise when limbs are being tensed and fall during deep relaxation.

• As attention to breathing is a feature of most muscular approaches, the hazards of hyperventilation should be taken into consideration. Some people may feel anxious when concentrating on trying to control their breathing, thus running the risk of hyperventilating. This risk may be small, but it is worth remembering that should you feel uncomfortable just to 'release control' and allow your body to return to its normal breathing pattern. Habits that have become established over many years may be difficult to change initially and need careful attention.

• As stated, in the majority of cases, relaxation is conducive to overall health and wellbeing. If you are unsure regarding your own particular circumstances, please consult your doctor for advice.

• It is advised not to use relaxation exercises immediately before or during any activity which requires a high level of concentration, such as driving or operating machinery. Also if you have a tendency to fall asleep whilst listening to any guided relaxation exercises, do not use whilst having a bath.

Three steps to relaxation

1. Focus on your body, your breathing, relax your muscles

Allow yourself to be comfortable and close your eyes. Focus your attention on your body and relax any tension in each part of your body. Listen to your breathing and to the air flowing into and out of your body. Don't change your breathing pattern, just become aware of it.
Be aware of what's going on inside you. Where is your attention? Just let go of everything right now. Allow the thoughts and feelings to flow through your mind and body.
Allow your forehead to relax, your jaw, your mouth and tongue, stretch your body to release any tension. Let yourself relax and listen to your breathing.
Notice how your body is feeling…listen to your breathing…put your right hand on your stomach and your left hand over your chest… listen… and feel the breathing movements. Bring your awareness to your hands… move your hands and relax them… be aware of your feet…wriggle your toes and relax them... stretch your neck and hunch and relax your shoulders, release tension from your mouth, tongue and jaw… tense your whole body and relax it…

2. Reassure your mind

Begin to calm down and relax – you have nowhere to go, nothing to do, just relax and be comfortable with yourself and who you are. Say to yourself, "Everything is okay, just for this moment." Enjoy the moment.
Repeat to yourself – "I'm okay just as I am right now, just for this moment."
Shift your attention from thinking and doing, to feeling and just being…
Your body is now feeling relaxed…. Your thoughts calm… emotions are rested…
You are breathing more slowly and more peacefully… let that warm feeling of peace cover your whole body.

3. Visualise a bright light

Imagine a bright light entering the top of your head. It is a warm, bright, glowing light which soothes and relaxes you, removing all tension as it travels through your head, down your neck, across your shoulders, down your arms and through to your fingers.
The warm, bright, golden light travels down your spine, through your chest and stomach, down your legs, knees and through to your feet and toes. Let this warm, bright light enfold you, giving you a feeling of deep peace and relaxation. Allow your body to feel lighter, softer and calmer.
Enjoy the moment, enjoy the peace, enjoy the calm. Bring your attention back to your body, your breathing and to the room around you. Give yourself a few minutes to collect yourself, before you open your eyes.

To purchase a guided relaxation exercise, developed by the author, available on CD, please visit online shop www.completeharmony.yokaboo.com

REFLECTION

What has this exercise revealed to you?

How might you incorporate relaxation into your lifestyle?

Do by date: when might you do this?

8 The Champion

"I always knew there wasn't going to be anybody to help me and emotionally support me, that whatever I did I'd have to do on my own."

Jack Nicholson, American actor, film director, producer and writer

Dynamic, fearless protectors, 8s are strong, magnanimous and passionate, champions of the vulnerable, they consume life's experiences with gusto: they want to take charge of their world.

"Being an 8 when things are going well is the best, I have lots of energy, feel free and happy to take on anything… I do like to get things done and to be in charge… it's what makes life interesting."

The most obvious of the gut types, 8s harness the energy of the anger centre by activating challenges in order to master them and provide for their own. Core values for an 8 are likely to include: justice, challenge, passion and responsibility.

"…he makes a wonderfully loyal, generous, loving, attentive and supportive husband and the most caring dad and son."

8s have an inbuilt awareness of potential vulnerability, which drives them to assume control: they feel inherently responsible for the welfare of everyone and everything. They create their own sense of justice, based, not on external principles like 1s, but on rules they create and change, pragmatically, as they go in order to meet the needs of their group.
Their people/projects are their all consuming passions in life, for whom/which they will give their life's blood; courageous to the core, they do not shirk pain or injury, taking pride in their battle scars as testament to their courage. Gutsy, charismatic lawyers and leaders – they roll up their sleeves and get stuck in with the troops they deploy, be it in business or battlefield.

On a good day!

"He is without question, generous to a fault. You know where you are with him… he is loyal to family and friends and is a great ideas man. He is above all, passionate about everything he does."

Practical, decisive and direct, 8s have the power and the confidence to quite literally move mountains. They have a strong physical presence, which can be emphasized by actual physique: others are always aware of their readiness to take action and would turn to them instinctively in times of crisis and need. 8s engender belief. Nothing is impossible: they exude invincibility. 8s are indomitable, they **will** find a way.

"… there is always a way. When I feel in control… I am at my happiest and most energetic…. happy to discuss anything under the sun."

"… (he) expects everyone to do it his way, which of course is the right way. In our house there is a humorous phrase, with some truth: 'Daddy is always right!'"

"If the challenge allows me to help and support my family and friends or is in a good cause, then even better."

Whilst 1s may suffer neglect themselves in the service of their external principles, 8s champion **their** cause, by **their** rules, with a healthy sense of self respect ensuring that their own needs are met. This fuels a dynamic, charismatic, competitive leadership; they seek, not to charm, like 3s, but to bring others under their domain. They offer absolute protection… and demand complete alliance.

"She takes on the leadership role in …(her) professional career with comfort and ease."

On a bad day!

"I do find it very difficult to be involved with things where I don't get the opportunity to have an impact and would usually walk away from those situations rather than play a supporting role."

"I like to take the initiative and lead from the front even though sometimes this can cause friction."

Inspirationally forthright - models of healthy assertiveness when in balance - when feeling out of control, 8s' need to challenge and take charge drives them to aggression and domination – they become the archetypal bully.

"When I am not in control of decisions... I don't function so well and ... I can become confrontational: things become a test of will which sometimes leads to me losing my temper."

In their determination to avoid vulnerability or any display of weakness, 8s can become ruthless, vengeful and possessive, savagely demolishing power they perceive as threatening, attempting to annihilate opposition, grinding it under the boot.

"I get irritable and can explode... or I can get frustrated with others. These outbursts can be scary for those who don't have any contact with 8s and those who don't understand, this is just part of being me."

The anger of the gut is overt and unleashed in unhealthy 8s: their bullish behaviour shows no consideration or awareness of others' needs – they are insensitive to the impact of their aggression on others, who tread on eggshells around them. Their view of people becomes polarized, a 'You're either with me or against me' mentality. Explosive and destructive, their unpredictable outbursts ultimately drive their own people away. Signs of independent challenge from them can then trigger covert, manipulative tactics as an attempt to re-establish control. The 8's overwhelming desire to protect by possession can lead to total isolation.

"It was so sad to watch, he adored them, but he couldn't let them go. The more he tried to bring them back, the more they ran away. He smothered them and in the end they couldn't bear to be around him."

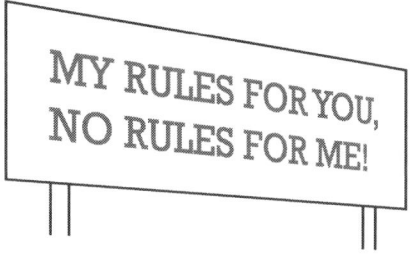

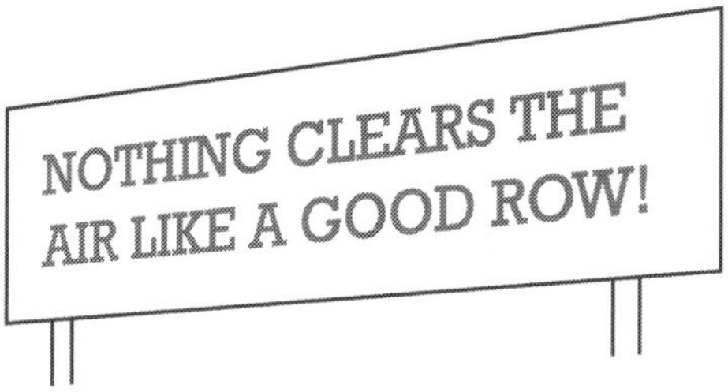

Finding a safe place to be vulnerable releases huge tenderness and warmth, enabling 8s to acknowledge and manage their need to connect with others on equal terms, activating and directing the forces of life to tremendous effect.

"My dad would come across as overbearing but never uncaring. He was our protector, our rock and he fixed everything."

"She is a force of nature, if she wants something doing, she makes it happen."

The gorilla is the epitome of the 8:
Fiercely protective of their group, from whom they demand absolute loyalty, gorillas are both deeply tender and gentle towards their young, and explosively aggressive towards any who challenge their power.

Core values for an 8 are likely to include:
justice, challenge, passion and responsibility.

8s supercharge our expectations of ourselves and of life; their example empowers us to be the masters of our own destiny.

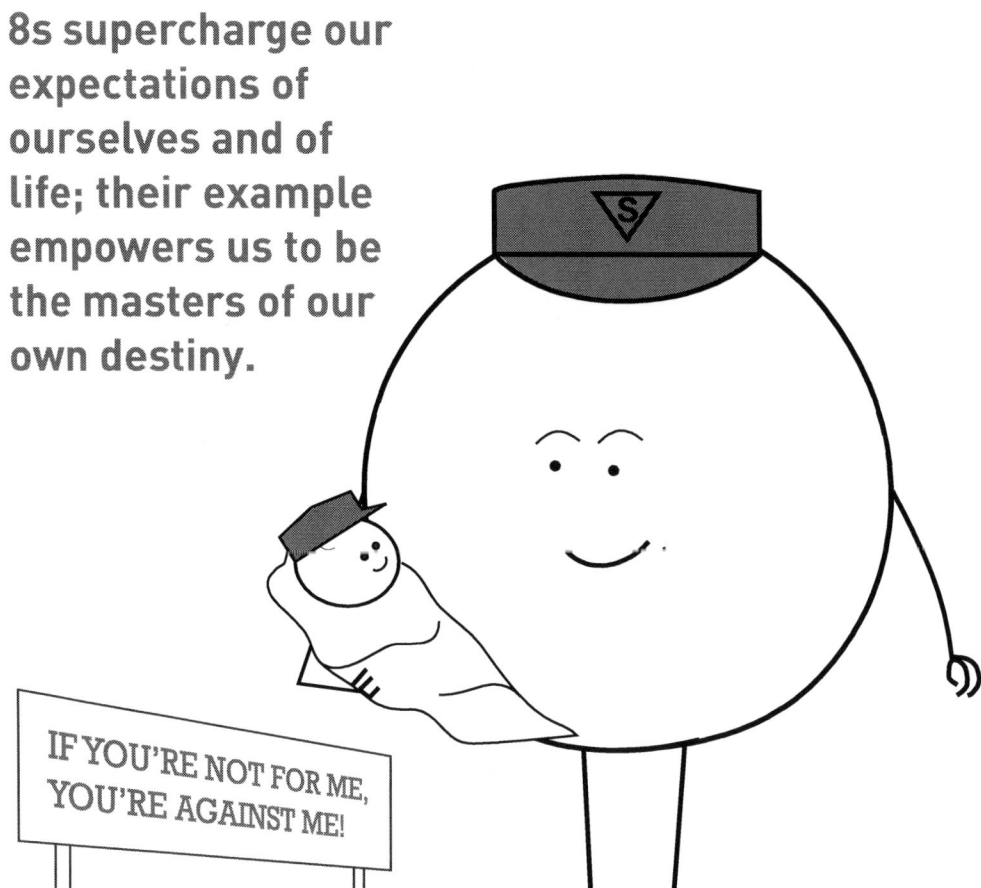

Coaching technique: Perceptual positioning

Interactions are at their best when those involved understand each other's perspectives. The Enneagram gives particular insight into the different maps from which different types are likely to be operating. This exercise has specific value for every type, as it invites us to explore tricky situations from three different perspectives: the perspective of 'self', of the 'other' and of an objective 'observer', in order to really appreciate these maps. Inviting 8s to step out of the perspective of 'self' can have major impact: it is important for them to feel strong and in control, but in doing so they may not have considered their potentially domineering effect on others.

Most other types will tend to have a habitual perspective: 2s and 9s, for different reasons, will tend to be so aware of others' needs that they will forget to consider their own; 4s and 1s, with 8s will be more likely to be focused on their own perspectives, 5s will tend to stay in the 'observer' perspective, avoiding connection with the emotions of the interaction. For each type, considering the situation from two other perspectives can bring enlightening awareness.

To activate the three perspectives:
First, pick an interaction which did not go as smoothly as you would have liked: one which would offer you real benefit if you could see it differently.

Then, take a few moments, possibly with your eyes closed, to imagine the scene, **from your own perspective**, as vividly as possible using all your senses.

Sight: Visualize all the details as clearly as you can, what does the other person look like? What expressions and body language are you seeing?

Hearing: Tune into the tones of voice, the speeds and volumes and how they come across to you; listen for your internal voice: what are you thinking as the interaction proceeds?

Feeling: Feel as fully as you can the emotional content of the interaction: what it is like to be with this other person; what you feel about the other person; how you feel about yourself and the relationship.

Then freeze the interaction. Notice what you have learned about yourself and the other person. Store this learning internally.

YOU CAN'T MAKE AN OMELETTE WITHOUT BREAKING EGGS!

Now repeat the exercise **from the perspective of the other**, stepping right into the other person, seeing yourself through his/her eyes, hearing yourself through his/her ears, feeling, as best you can, what the other person is feeling and how you feel about yourself, as the interaction unfolds.
Freeze the interaction, notice any learning, store the learning internally.

Finally, step into the experience **from the perspective of a benevolent observer** who is neutral. See your whole interaction through the observer's eyes, notice the body language and expressions from this, neutral perspective. Listen to what is said and how it is said. Become aware of how this relationship has developed through past exchanges; notice any patterns or repetitions.

Freeze the interaction for the last time. Store your observations and learning. Reflect on any new awareness.

As you consider this information, think about what you could say, do or feel differently that would not transgress your beliefs and values and yet could shift this relationship onto a different level.

Consider changes which could have been made. What impact might changing body language, tone of voice, or words spoken have? This might be a very small change or a larger one. It might be one thing or several things.

Some of the things to consider might be:

- a new posture or gestures,
- moving closer to the other person or further away,
- moving next to them or in front of them,
- changing the look on your face,
- using new words or a different tone of voice,
- or just feeling differently about the other person or yourself.

Think of the next time that you are likely to be with this person. Know that this time you will have some new behaviours to try out. Imagine trying out these new possibilities, noticing how this affects the other person, changing his/her behaviour and improving the quality of the interaction. Store this learning, ready to use whenever you choose to.

REFLECTION

What has this exercise revealed to you?

What actions could you take as a result of your learning?

Do by date: when might you do this?

9 The Peacemaker

*"If you want to make peace with your enemy,
you have to work with your enemy.
Then he becomes your partner."*
"I dream of an Africa which is at peace with itself."

**Nelson Mandela, South African anti-apartheid activist,
President of South Africa from 1994-1999**

Easy-going, tranquil, natural facilitators, 9s are gentle, grounded and very self-contained; maintaining a calm equilibrium in life, they create a safe space for others. Subconsciously, they want connection: with themselves and/or with people and with the world around them.

"When in a healthy place ... Everything feels in balance, calm and the world is a wonderful place... I can support anyone through the most difficult times."

9s are the least obvious of the gut types: driven by anger and yet, unlike the 8s and 1s, where anger is evident, the 9's personality is built around the need to **avoid** showing anger. Whilst 8s and 1s overtly attempt to control the world around them, 9s take control one step further: their subconscious aim is to prevent life from having emotional impact on them - they attempt to control themselves and their environment to minimise this impact. Core values for the 9 are likely to include: harmony, peace of mind, compassion and flexibility.

"... I don't like over-enthusiasm, nor do I like negativity. I often try to counter-balance these moods in others around me so that there is a chilled-out atmosphere."

A high-functioning 9 is an unexpected powerhouse, a skilled, instinctual negotiator, catalysing transformation even in the most extreme of circumstances. A healthy 9 will instantly evoke trust. This enables people to communicate openly and honestly, with someone who can dispassionately embrace charged and challenging situations without judgement whilst preserving emotional balance.

"He is cool, calm and collected, utterly unflappable, dealing with the most difficult situations with such apparent calm – it keeps everyone else level. It's so reassuring, somehow we just know everything is going to be okay."

On a good day!

This warm, empathic and patient demeanour makes 9s very easy to be around, they will generally have a wisdom about them - not knowledge-based like the 5, but an instinctive, emotional 'knowing' without need for logic. Receptive 9s seek harmony through understanding all perspectives - active listeners, they will diffuse tension and promote reconciliation.

*"I find myself able to talk about absolutely **anything** with her – I feel so safe – I know that she's not going to over react, she doesn't need to butt in, she gives me space to unravel my thoughts and my feelings and I know she is never going to judge me."*

When centred and balanced, 9s nurture health in any or all of its forms: physical, mental and spiritual. They have a unique desire for a greater connection with universal intelligence - they search for meaning, they are drawn to the spiritual, with a powerful desire to feel at one with nature, the environment, with themselves.

"... Everything is effortless, fulfilling, I feel so energised and enthusiastic: motivated, full of confidence, I don't know how I could ever feel better! I can achieve anything!"

On a bad day!

The serene exterior of the 9 belies the immense energy used to keep emotions under control - the analogy of the swan, gliding apparently effortlessly with frantic paddling feet inches below the surface comes to mind. Exhaustion is a feature of 9s; keeping the see-saw of life in balance to avoid the ups and downs along the way is massively draining. 9s have a major need for 'down-time' away from others, where they can completely let go of the strain of buffering their own and others' emotions.

"I feel overloaded and out of control: all of those plates on sticks are about to come crashing down... My body feels heavy and so tired. I have trouble thinking, I want to curl up somewhere warm and safe, I don't want to socialise - I just want to sleep."

9s avoid being affected by the dramas of life because these might lead to conflict: they can become bumbling and oblivious, procrastinating and verbose in their attempts to bubble wrap the rough edges of life. They will vividly remember times when their own or others' loss of emotional balance has threatened their connection.

"Extremes of emotion cause him to feel overwhelm and disrupts his no-fuss, relaxed persona."

What some 9s will be unaware of however is that this desire to maintain connection derives from a stronger need. Conflict threatens to unleash that which they fear most: their own, unacknowledged rage.

"I ... let things build up ... where they magnify to the point of no return and I lose my temper ..."

9s can go to extremes in their attempts to avoid this rage. They can become sluggish, apathetic, overly accommodating - they tolerate too much for fear of 'rocking the boat' or they withdraw to avoid stress. The healthy need to rest and recharge becomes an overwhelming laziness as the 9 struggles to manage energy levels. Numb and nebulous, they can lose touch with their feelings; they dare not express opinions so they suppress them, or hide them in interminable ramblings; they sit on the fence, maintaining the status quo but at a cost.

"... He will quietly do his own thing and get his way, in a quiet, non-disruptive manner."

At some point however, the strain begins to tell and the stubborn, resistant, passive aggression of the 9 emerges, although overt anger may still be well hidden. Pushed further still, control may snap and volcanic rage erupts. For 9s who have experienced this, it is the 'Incredible Hulk' syndrome - "Don't make me angry, you wouldn't like me when I'm angry!"

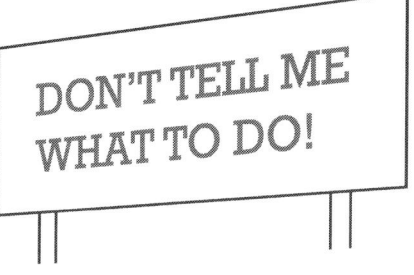

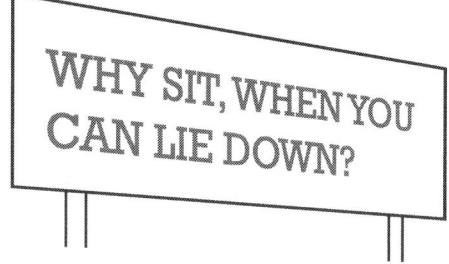

A 9's passion for peace is second to none and when confident to harness the power of the gut centre, 9s have the gift to go 'where angels fear to tread', absorbing the most explosive situations, diffusing contentious situations, dissolving conflict.

"Ever the diplomat, she takes on conflicts with apparent ease, negotiating powerfully without losing ground and somehow preserving, even enhancing, the relationship. It is quite stunning to watch."

The bear is the epitome of the 9:
Soft, affectionate with its young, lethargic and lumbering, the bear appears gentle and appealing - the archetypal cuddly toy, but its aggression, when provoked, is powerful and deadly.

Core values for the 9 are likely to include: harmony, peace of mind, compassion and flexibility.

The compassion of the 9 reminds us that relationships are paramount; they invite us to honour the dignity of life, by seeing beyond behaviours to embrace the spirit within.

Coaching technique: Health and wellbeing wheel

The health and wellbeing wheel is a fantastic exercise for anyone who neglects their own wellbeing. In particular - 9s to maintain control, and 2s to aquire love, can neglect themselves, sacrificing balance and harmony in order to accommodate others. See how balanced your wellbeing is at the moment. This is an excellent exercise to revisit periodically.

Score your sense of satisfaction with each aspect of your health & wellbeing. Regarding the centre of the wheel as 0 and the outer edge as 10, rank your level of satisfaction with each area by drawing a straight or curved line to create a new outer edge. Identify areas you wish to improve. Determine what actions you will take to improve your scores.

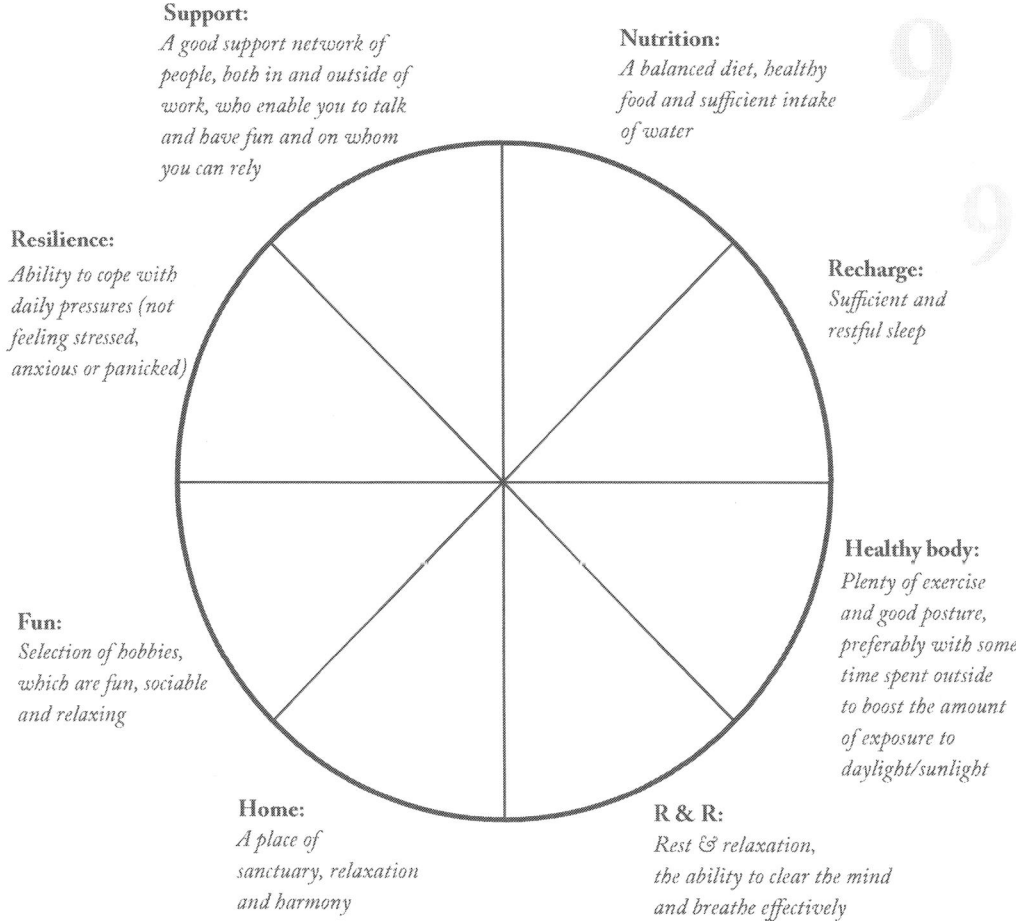

Support:
A good support network of people, both in and outside of work, who enable you to talk and have fun and on whom you can rely

Nutrition:
A balanced diet, healthy food and sufficient intake of water

Resilience:
Ability to cope with daily pressures (not feeling stressed, anxious or panicked)

Recharge:
Sufficient and restful sleep

Healthy body:
Plenty of exercise and good posture, preferably with some time spent outside to boost the amount of exposure to daylight/sunlight

Fun:
Selection of hobbies, which are fun, sociable and relaxing

Home:
A place of sanctuary, relaxation and harmony

R & R:
Rest & relaxation, the ability to clear the mind and breathe effectively

REFLECTION

What has this exercise revealed to you?

What actions could you take to improve your health and wellbeing?

Do by date: when might you do this?

1 The Reformer

"A principle is the expression of perfection, and as imperfect beings like us cannot practise perfection, we devise every moment limits of its compromise in practice."

Mahatma Ghandi, led India to independence, inspired movements for non-violence, civil rights and freedom across the world

Conscientious, principled, scrupulously honest, 1s are 'big picture' visionaries. Loyal and idealistic, they will work tirelessly and dependably; they want to make the world a better place.

"I am the only person I know ... who plays the (card) game (cheat) and tells the truth or giggles stupidly when I tell a lie."

1s are the last of the gut centres, seeking control. Whilst the 8s approach this by overt challenge and 9s by avoidance, 1s desire perfection; they are bound by their code of ethics - they **have** to "do the right thing and do it right", no matter what the cost. Core values for the 1 are likely to include: honesty, integrity, truth and trust.

".... (I was) stopped by the police for speeding, on finishing the conversation I said 'Thank you'! Thank you for being given a ticket, ... (it) was the right thing to do!"

"He has strong views ... about things ... He honours all agreements and if he commits himself to doing something – it will happen!"

Industrious, disciplined and hard working, 1s strive to achieve the highest of standards, as this allows them to feel in control of their world.

"I can be productive, organised and focused – particularly with regards to my working life. I want to be the best that I can be and work hard in order to achieve this."

On a good day!

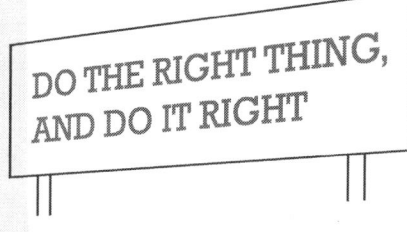

When emotionally balanced, 1s command respect; their strength of purpose is inspirational, making them visionary leaders: they instinctively know what to do. They shoulder responsibility when few others would, committing themselves utterly to 'the cause', be it great or small.

"...he... takes responsibilities very, very seriously...he believes that all of us –... are fully responsible for our lives...He has a heightened sense of right and wrong..... Honourable intentions and behaviour are paramount. ...These 'life rules' are rigorously applied to himself and therefore his life is tough and stressful. He is very hard on himself and expects other people to be equally principled."

Vulnerability in others evokes immense warmth, generosity and kindness from a 1. 1s will move heaven and earth for those in need – not in order to feel needed themselves, as with the 2, but because it is the right thing to do.

"He applies his 'life rules' with care, to ensure he is fair to everyone. He ... feels it is his moral duty to give his best to everyone. He also wants the best for everyone and is constantly seeking to improve how life is conducted."

The strength and reliability of the 1 hides their own vulnerability; others may never guess the insecurities and troubles they shoulder, these are shared only with those in their small circle of trust, they play their cards very close to their chest.

Trust is paramount to a 1. When they are "allowed to be naughty" their wicked sense of humour emerges, with keen wit and an unexpected ability to laugh at themselves.

On a bad day!

"... I only feel that I can really let my hair down ... when I'm with people that I truly trust and I feel won't judge me. ... if anyone I trust lets me down I find it very hard to trust them completely again."

1s have a subconscious **need** to be right, which is driven by an incessant inner critic which torments them continuously. Whilst other types may experience this inner critic intermittently, there is absolutely no let up for a 1 - it is never good enough. Serious, even severe, when out of balance, 1s can become harsh and ascetic in their approach to life, particularly work; scant in praise, rigid and uncompromising, they find it incredibly hard to relax completely and be frivolous - it just feels 'wrong'. 1s are constantly worrying: judging themselves and finding themselves lacking, this makes them super-sensitive to anything that remotely hints at criticism coming at them from others, particularly in company.

"Getting things right is so important to a 1 that ... (they) live in a constant state of tension."

"... this drive to be the best that I can be means that I can feel like I am not good enough and I always see the imperfections in my work... It is easy to be overly harsh on myself and criticise myself too heavily."

This "drive to be the best" is not, as in the 3 make up, for external recognition, but is a search for approval, to be deemed 'good enough'. The internal, unattainably high standards driving the 1 to constant, 'nit-picking' judgement of self, externalises when out of balance - "I should" and "I ought" rapidly spill out to become "**You** should... **You** ought" which may not be verbalised but is palpable in their body language and tone of voice.

"If I have been working alongside him, I can quickly fall into feeling disapproved of... I try to keep in mind he is only worrying because of his desire to do the right thing."

1s oscillate between believing in their own 'perfection' - "... If I want a job done properly I have to do it myself" - and being devastated by evidence of their own failings. This polarised view of life can, when out of balance, skew their judgements - compromising the very integrity and truthfulness they prize so dearly. Inflexible and self-righteous, they are very black and white where key values are concerned.

"He has struggled to understand why other people do not apply the same moral fortitude to their work. He doesn't ask any more of a colleague than he would ask of himself – but he is a very demanding task-master."

Conflict troubles 1s deeply. Unhealthy 1s are torn between blazing anger with anything that fails to meet their standards and the overwhelming inability to express that anger healthily - losing one's temper is just not right. This suppressed, opinionated anger will be evident to others - they become intense, even puritanical - the 1s will imagine that they have succeeded in hiding it completely from view.

"... although I know I've got a right to be angry I am so afraid of letting it go that I just seethe. ... I feel like a pressure cooker that hasn't let off enough steam.... I'm healthier when I physically work off my tension (preferably) ... with a pair of boxing gloves on my hands."

As gut types, 1s will only show their vulnerability and warmth to trusted confidants. With these people they can show breathtaking humility - they so want to do it right. Once reassured that they are good enough, they can make peace with imperfection, unlocking deep compassion, which enables them to become a zealous power for change, they literally re-form their world.

"My husband is … a knight on a quest"

"I think that in many ways a 1 personality is a very humble soul who simply seeks to provide the best quality service possible to all people.'

The honeybee is the epitome of the 1:
Hardworking and busy, the bumblebee, ever loyal, will make the ultimate sacrifice for the greater good - whilst we are wary of their wrath, their productivity drives improvement: it is fundamental to life itself.

Core values for the 1 are likely to include:
honesty, integrity, truth and trust.

These strategic leaders show inspirational dedication to their vision of how the world should be - they raise the bar for us all.

Coaching technique: Support system

It is important for us all to have a support system, remember that, 'A problem shared is a problem halved'. We have friends and contacts who are often willing to help and support, but sometimes we don't feel like bothering them, or 'being a nuisance'.

This exercise is useful for everyone, but particularly for 1s who, when out of balance, feel they have to do everything for themselves and can struggle to delegate. 2s may also benefit specifically from this as they are likely to feel compelled to be everyone else's support network, but will avoid acknowledging a need for support of their own.

Support networks are vital and keeping a note of your network will help when the time comes to call on someone. Make a note for yourself under the following headings.

Someone on whom I can rely in a crisis
Someone who helps me feel good about myself
Someone with whom I can be totally myself
Someone who will give me feedback in a way that feels supportive
Someone to whom I can talk when I am worried
Someone with whom I can have fun

Check to see if you are overly reliant on very few people. Expand your list wherever possible. Imagine the people on this list were unavailable, to whom would you turn then?

If you find this difficult, it may be an indication that you have type 1 tendencies.

My support system

Someone on whom I can rely in a crisis:

Someone who helps me feel good about myself:

Someone with whom I can be totally myself:

Someone who will give me feedback in a way that feels supportive:

Someone to whom I can talk when I am worried:

Someone with whom I can have fun:

REFLECTION

What has this exercise revealed to you?

What actions could you take to strengthen your support network?

Do by date: when might you do this?

There's more to life than painting by numbers

Painting by numbers

As we said at the start, life is so much more than painting by numbers! You may now have a clear picture of your number and even the numbers of others, but this is not a limitation to a simple line-defined shape - quite the opposite in fact - it is an invitation to something far richer.

To enhance your understanding at this point, the following may be helpful:

I know my type, how do I make the most of who I am?

Some types do tend to recognise themselves more swiftly, the crucial thing now is to understand the message we started with and the title of this chapter. This is NOT who you are! This is a set of behaviours. In 'The Enneagram – Going Deeper,' the second book in this series, we will show you how to utilise your understanding of the Enneagram to bring the best out of your personality type.

I could be one of 2 or 3 different types, how do I work it out?

As a starting point, this is where returning to the chapter on the three centres can be helpful. Clarifying the main driving emotion is the foundation for pinpointing our types. Looking deeper, are you driven by a feeling of hurt or shame and a need for love/attention? Or fear and a need for safety? Or anger and a need to control?

In 'The Enneagram – Going Deeper,' we will take you through the different processes needed to sort 'look-alikes' more thoroughly, sieving the types according to their responses to stresses and needs, their connections with each other and the probable 'look-alike' behaviours each type is most likely to adopt.

I'm not sure which type I am, help?

This can happen – remember, we can all do all of the behaviours – it's the underlying motivations we are seeking and we may well have done a good job of hiding them from ourselves. Start by eliminating any types with which you do not resonate strongly. This should narrow the field; then re-read the sections on the remaining types. If you find that you resonate with just about all the types, finding it difficult to eliminate any, re-read the chapter on the 9, the Peacemaker, as 9s are most likely to adopt every other type's behaviours in order to maintain harmony.

If you find that you resonate with 2 neighbouring types, this is known as a 'Wing effect'. It will probably indicate that one of the types is your fundamental base and the other influences it strongly. If the 2 types are in different centres, re-read the section on the three centres and gauge which centre resonates the best.

I think I know someone else's type – how can I be sure?

Just a reminder, it is never our place to type another person although it is human nature to do just that. If you are noticing behaviour that indicates a particular type, remember that you will bring your own filters into the mix – you may find everyone looking rather like your type because you are drawing that out of them, for example, or you may imagine that anyone displaying a particular emotion is bringing up your own nemesis, which leads to inaccurate typing as a result.

What works best is to notice the behaviours and use Enneagram understanding to enhance your interactions, remembering that there may be very different subconscious drivers operating.

I work/live with someone who is very out of balance. How do I help them?

The Enneagram shows us very powerfully the reasons why another person's behaviours are so difficult – they 'push our (personality) buttons'. This work reminds us that it is never about 'fixing' anyone else. It is always about helping yourself to regain and retain balance even in difficult situations.
Key questions to ask in these circumstances are: 'What can this person teach me about myself?' and 'What is my need here, and how can I meet it?'

Do some types get on better than others?

We like to describe the interactions between types as a dance. Some combinations create more spark, more passion – one combination might play out like an Argentinean Tango, another might tend to run more smoothly with Viennese Waltz-like grace. Another again might never be tempted onto the floor, enjoying the scene from the seats.

If the interactions in your life were a series of dances, which ones are playing out in your life just now?

Reflecting on the vast number of different dances, we can see the range of possibilities. This helps us to remember that there are no 'better' or 'worse' dances. Each one can be an absolute delight. Equally, each combination of types has a gift to bring. The Enneagram invites us to embrace the things we subconsciously (or consciously) avoid in others, to become more rounded, more complete in our encompassing of all types, both in the personal and professional arenas.

Thoughts to ponder...

You will now have a sense of the richness of the Enneagram and the reason we liken it to an impressionist painting. The lines within the Enneagram are blurred, the colours merge and blend - nature and nurture and the rich influence of environment, the links and connections between the types allow so much movement, such power to choose and change and evolve.

But more than all of this, the awareness you have now – even if it is only partial – of personality drivers enables you to *choose differently*. It can be powerful to just ask - how would a 7 handle this? Or a 3? How would I like to handle this? Step out of the subconscious mould which may have limited you in the past and allow yourself to play it differently.

Author Biographies

Amanda Maney is an Assistant Head Teacher with over 20 years' experience working with primary school children. She is also an accredited Life Coach and an Advanced EFT practitioner, Matrix Re-imprinting practitioner with training also in Solution Focused Brief Therapy, NLP and Journey Therapy.

Amanda has found Enneagram wisdom invaluable in her coaching-based approach to enabling and personalising children's learning and also in her wider work: training, coaching and facilitating teams and individuals.

'Know thyself' is central to her approach - self awareness creates the springboard for children and adults alike. Amanda's prime directive is personal empowerment: creating success by synergy and harnessing enthusiasm to expand potential, with children and adults alike. Amanda and her husband live in the North West of England which has been home to her since leaving her birthplace, London in 1986.

Rachel Watson is a successful lifestyle and business coach and trainer. She has 20-years' experience of working within the corporate arena and more than a decade as a professional coach.

Rachel is an accredited Executive Coach with the Association for Coaching, an accredited NLP and Stress Management practitioner, accredited AAMET EFT Advanced practitioner, Matrix Re-imprinting practitioner, Reiki Master, and RMT provider, a member of Mensa and a member of The Institute for Learning.

Rachel is passionate about the importance of wellbeing. As a working mother of 4 grown up children, she knows firsthand the challenges of juggling life demands and a rewarding career, whilst raising a family. Rachel lives in the North West of England with her husband.

Further endorsements

This is a fascinating and worthwhile read for anyone interested in self exploration and personal development. I really enjoyed analysing my own personality and I couldn't help but delve into the personality traits of those who are near and dear! It's a great addition to my enlightenment tool box!

Lynn Blades, BA, PCC
Life Skills Curator, Wonder PL

Everyone should read this book – and I mean EVERYONE. The writers inspire us to see that we are all equally worthy human beings who can learn to appreciate the joys of different personality types. Applying these two key ideas alone to relationships whether in the workplace, at school or at home is a great starting point for creating personal success. This book also provides clever and thought provoking information about personality types that transcends any simple systems of defining who we are but is easy to read and understand. Undeniably useful and potentially life–changing, I wish I had known about the Enneagram when I was younger as I am sure its wisdom would have enriched my life and it might have saved me from some troublesome moments too!

Sharon Ginnis, Education Trainer and Consultant, co author with Paul Ginnis,
"Covering the Curriculum with Stories"

So what next?

The Enneagram – Going Deeper will cover:

- a summary of key avoidances, communication styles, pitfalls and strengths, the ways the types react to stress and need,

- the links and dynamics between types – why some connections seem stronger and more intuitive than others,

- the 'Wing' effects – how the types are affected by the personalities on either side,

- the variants of each type – the source of our life's 'juice',

- 'Dos and Don'ts' – some tips to help bring the best out of the different types.

Notes

Notes

Printed in Great Britain
by Amazon